Autism in a Nutshell?

Okay…Maybe a Nuthouse
101 Reasons Our Family is SOOO "Special"

Suzanne M. Mitchell

For my babies. I love you more than a million words could ever express. You are my heart and soul, forever and always.

Table of Contents

Acknowledgments

Thank you to my family, and everyone that has ever fallen in love with my beautiful boy. He is quite amazing, and so are you.

Introduction

Hi...We are The Mitchell Family. I am Suzanne. My husband Darin and I have been together since 1989, when I was just sixteen years old (now I'm 41...yikes). He was the new bass player in by older brother's band, and I was the cool "rocker" chick.

Our mutual love of rock-n-roll is what brought us together, and our deep love for each other and our little family is what has kept us going strong all these years.

We were married in 1998, and have two beautiful children. Joey is thirteen, and Shayna is ten. Joey has severe autism. He is not very verbal, is not potty trained, and can be quite unpredictable at times.

We are not your average family. People often ask me what our life is like, and I always find it difficult to explain. If I had to put our life into a nutshell, I'd have to say that it is full of insanity, patience, inspiration, persistence and love.

But if you REALLY want to know what life is like for one crazy autism mama bear...please read on.

Suzanne M. Mitchell

1. Maybe we'll discover that Vaseline is the cure for autism?

It was a relatively calm evening in our house, Joey was playing quietly in his room, and Shayna was watching a movie. I think I had just finished cleaning up after dinner, when I decided to go check on my boy... (maybe it was a little "too quiet").

So I went upstairs, and immediately noticed a strange scent in the air. I looked at my son (I think he was 8 or 9 at the time) and saw that the entire area around his mouth, and part of his head were not only oddly shiny, but he was holding a large sized jar of scented Vaseline, which was almost empty.

Smelling his breath, in combination with the lack of evidence in any other location, quickly lead me to the conclusion that he had eaten most of it!! OMG!!! Total panic. I grabbed the phone, started to call 911, and then hung up to call poison control. Poison control told me that he would be fine, but he might have some tummy issues.

I was so relieved, but I guess in my earlier state of panic, I hadn't looked at the caller ID when I was on the other line with poison control. Apparently if you hang up on 911, they call you back and send out an officer. Hmmm. Oops.

Sooo, as Darin and I were giving Joey a bath, and just starting to calm down, the doorbell rang. Shayna peeked through the window (I think she was around 5 at the time) and yelled upstairs, "Mama!! The police are here!!" Holy moly!! What a night!!

From that day forward, both upstairs bathrooms stay locked when we are not using them. Good times!! :-))

Oh and by the way, after the excitement was over, the optimist in me was totally hoping that maybe we had accidentally stumbled onto the fact that ingesting large amounts of Vaseline cures autism (kind of like the "You got chocolate in my peanut butter! You got peanut butter in my chocolate!" Reese's Peanut Butter Cup commercials of my youth), but unfortunately, that was not the case.

2. Taking my boy to the grocery store...

My son is much more verbal in the grocery store than he is anywhere else, so as complicated as it makes the experience, I feel it is important for him to come with me sometimes.

He will not only name most foods that he wants, but he will fully intend to taste each one before we are to the end of our shopping trip. It's great motivation for him to use words.

Let me tell you though, he is not what I would call a "neat eater", so I tend to walk through the store, encouraging him to verbally say what he wants instead of just grabbing, as I stick little bites directly into his mouth so he doesn't make a mess. I do this as I am making sure to grab all of the other items that we need in that aisle.

Then, the more peaceful section. The moment that I get a little break from the constant little bites. Any guesses?? The produce aisle!!! Yay!! He will take an apple or an orange and eat happily for a few minutes (if it's an orange, he will just go ahead and eat it like an apple, skin and all. But he doesn't drop a bit... go figure.)

Now, the part that keeps me on my toes in the produce section is the old, "pick it up, lick it, and try to put it back without my mom noticing trick." Yuck!! I have purchased more pre- licked cucumbers, peppers, melons etc. than anyone else in the land!! He is so fast!!

As we round the corners, I am always on the look- out for two possible enemies. The first would be a whining or screaming toddler, and the second would be some sort of display with either balloons or strings or anything of that nature (especially the dreaded pool noodles display...He LOVES those!!)

Unfortunately, the screaming child will often result in an immediate agitation and possible aggression, likely leading to our early exit from the store, while the display with strings etc. would only mean that a meltdown may be coming soon, but only when I make him put the stuff back. At least I'd have a few minutes to form a plan of action with enemy #2. Both are possible landmines for us.

OK... our cart is full, it's time for the checkout adventure. The beeping, the waiting, the other people in line, the candy display, the conveyor belt that he may want to touch, other people's carts with food he likes, telling the cashier which packages are opened so they don't spill...It is quite a relaxing experience for me, I tell ya!! Ha!!

If at any time we don't have to leave the store in a mad dash without our stuff, it has been a successful trip. Yay!!! I hope I remembered to buy wine!! :-))

3. Dinner Time!!

When the kids get home from school, the kitchen definitely becomes my home base for the next several hours. It's all about food. My daughter gets home first, and usually she'll have a snack or two before my son gets home.

When he comes in that front door, he heads straight for the kitchen! Pantry, fridge. Pantry, fridge. Pantry, fridge. Holy food tornado, Batman! I let him choose what he wants, but sometimes he is in such a food finding frenzy, that I cannot even keep up with him.

Within a few minutes, he has usually settled on something, and is sitting at the kitchen table eating. This peaceful moment however, is often quite short lived, and normally, he will be back up and rummaging through the kitchen shortly.

Joey is very verbal when it comes to food, but unless you know him, you may not always know what he is talking about. For example, one of his favorite snacks is Ramen noodles. But when he asks for them, he calls them "Jim". "I want Jim please". He has said this for years. I have no idea where it came from, but we all know what he means. Pretty funny.

Then there's "carrot". Now you would think that this is self-explanatory, but that is rarely the case in our house. "Carrot" is what Joey says for a roll with butter. Why? I have NO idea, but I'll take language and communication any way I can get it!!

Anyway, the insatiable snacking is tapering off a little by this point, and I can get dinner started (Yes, "Jim" is usually just an appetizer). Once my boy sees that dinner will likely be in the near future, he will find something else to do for a little while (walking through the kitchen peeking in on dinner's progress every so often).

This is usually about the time that my hubby gets home from work. Shayna will go running and yelling "Daddy!!" while Joey prefers a quieter entrance. He will give his high fives and a smile, but then head up to his room for a bit to get a break from the noise and hoopla.

Within a couple minutes, he's back downstairs asking for, "Chicken, please." He doesn't always mean chicken, but it's usually the first thing that he'll say. Now depending on what I'm making, he might say different things. For example, if he sees something being cooked on the stove, he'll often say, "I want hot please". Now this one I get, because I have told him a million times while I'm cooking that, "This is hot".

Okay…Dinner is ready and it's time to eat. Because my

sweet boy is known to be a "stuffer" (too much food in his mouth at once and not enough chewing), and because of a trip to the ER when he was 4 when he choked on a bite of steak, I usually monitor his bites as he's eating meat and/or noodles/rice, having him take sips of water as we go. It makes it a little challenging for me to eat what others might consider "normally", but as with many things in my life, "normal" is not a priority. Ha!!

4. I want Wiggles please...

Thirteen plus years ago when my son was a baby, I was always on the look-out for something cute and fun that we could enjoy together. (Actually, I am still that way). Well, along came "The Wiggles", an Australian foursome that wrote and performed many catchy tunes, and paired them with other great characters on an entertaining and harmless TV show. Joey LOVED them, and honestly, I liked them too.

When he was 3, we took both kids to see them live, and I was actually excited to hear certain songs…I know it's weird, but we were really into them. Well, it turns out that it is a REALLY lucky thing that I don't find them horribly annoying, because we have listened to and/or watched, some sort of Wiggly something EVERY SINGLE DAY for the last thirteen years!! Wowza!!

He still loves their classics. I know all of the words backwards and forwards, and I still don't hate them. I actually find myself singing their songs without noticing (when it's not even on…and sometimes when Joey isn't even home!!) I'm not the only one either. Yep…We sure are an interesting bunch!!

5. Let's play outside!!

My hubby and I are outside people. We have always loved camping, fishing, walks in the woods, the beach etc. since we met (I was 16 when we started dating…approximately a million years ago, and way before marriage and children). When going off for a weekend in our dating years, the ultimate campsite was always what we were looking for…that private wooded lot with beautiful trees and privacy, a cool fire pit, etc.

Well, when we found our house, I swear I heard angels singing when I first peeked through the fence and saw the yard. I had not even seen the inside yet, and I was sold. We have the best campsite in the world, and there also happens to be a beautiful house that came with it!! Hee Hee.

Not surprisingly, we have passed on our love of the outdoors to our kids. Joey in particular. He can play outside for hours and hours. He loves to swim, swing, jump on the trampoline, play on the hammock, etc. (I will include the pool in its own little section, because he LOVES that the most).

To the naked or unsuspecting eye, our yard may not appear to have any "special" modifications specifically necessary for our beautiful boy, but I will share a few of them with you here.

Let's start with the trampoline. Our trampoline is only about one foot off the ground. When we got it, we bought it from a neighbor that was moving. She had it set up without the legs, and I thought that was brilliant!! Totally safe and fun, and no ugly and most likely not "Joey proof" net was necessary.

At the time, our kids were only about five and two years old, so it worked out really well. Now that they are getting older, they kind of hit the ground quickly when they try to jump in the middle. Joey, however, has learned to stay around the edge so he can still bounce. He runs around the edge of the circle, and still enjoys it tremendously.

We should probably get the bigger kind at this point, but I am still not sure that a safety net would keep my bouncing boy safe. That kid can get some serious air, and he would probably chew the net and peel it apart, rendering it useless.

On to the swing set. Again, at first glance, it may look normal, but a closer look will reveal a couple of "non-conventional" items. First, because our boy tends to have a taste for mud and dirt, (I know...eww) we have put pieces of indoor/outdoor carpeting under the swings where he would otherwise hang and feast on the yucky stuff.

Secondly, we have a very long piece of rope that is tied onto the swing set because he loves to stand there and twirl that thing for quite a while. Twirl, twirl, twirl and chew. Twirl, twirl, twirl and chew.

Then there's the hammock. Now most people think of a hammock as a place for relaxation. Not our Joey. He thinks of it as the most awesome piece of circus equipment ever invented. He does some crazy stuff on that thing. That's why we are on our third one or so, and why I always have to buy the extra durable two person type that can take a beating. There is a piece of indoor/outdoor carpet under the hammock as well. (Yep...eew again).

Lastly, any other hoses, strings, wires, etc. that may have to be outdoors, have to be either camouflaged, tied down, or hidden because he will become completely obsessed with playing with them. It makes for quite a challenge when we need to use a garden hose or plug something in!! Always an adventure!!

6. It's Potty Time / I know you knew your ABC's , why then won't you sing with me?? (anymore)

Oh, where do I even start on this one?…Heavy sigh. Pottying. Hmmm. OK, well when Joey was about two to two and a half, and maybe even for part of three, he was seemingly catching on to the whole potty training thing. He would go pee when I would sit him down, and sometimes he would even say "pee pee on the potty" when he actually had to go. He would poop in the potty fairly regularly at that time too, but only if I had the right timing.

Then came baby #2. My sweet little Shayna Bug. I started having what I now know were panic attacks soon after having my daughter. I didn't understand what was wrong with me, but I soon realized that it was not me or the new baby that I was concerned about…it was my Joey.

Denial is a powerful tool, and the concerns that I may have had about my son when I got pregnant with my daughter, were shoved deep down inside my soul until they reared their ugly heads in the form of panic attacks after giving birth. I thought I was going to die at any moment.. It was terrifying.

So now I guess I have to back up a little bit. I always knew that I would stay home with my babies when I had them. Thankfully, I was with my husband long enough before we got married, that I had already drilled that fact into his head as well. SOOO, we were married a little over two years when Joey was born.

It was amazing. I took him everywhere. I did everything with him. We were inseparable (literally inseparable if you ask my family…they say I wouldn't even let anybody else hold him. I don't remember it that way, but oh well...hee hee). We sang, we read, we played, we learned, it was a magical time for both of us. Of course at that time, I had no idea exactly how precious every tiny morsel of my teaching and his learning would be.

As time went by, he learned and sang tons of songs, he knew all of his colors, all of his letters, numbers, shapes, animals, etc. He would fill in the blank on the next line of a book, he would touch pictures and follow along. He would talk about his day when he got into his crib at night. We would hear him giving the highlights on the baby monitor…"Went to library, saw animals, fishies, swings, park", etc.

It was so cute. He would say "Hi, Mama!" when I came into his room to get him. He would ask for different things and was quite easy to understand. He loved it when I read to him, and then one day he didn't like it anymore.

I wish now that I had all of those wonderful moments recorded somewhere besides only in my head, heart and soul. I had no idea how absolutely precious and perfect those moments were. As any mother would assume, I thought this was the beginning of blossoming language, not the end.

As a stay at home mom, and just because of who I am, I definitely noticed that Joey began to "forget" things that I knew he had previously known. For quite a while, I was blaming myself , thinking maybe we hadn't sang a particular song for too long, or we hadn't read a certain book in a while. Why didn't he know these things anymore?

I was not sure what the heck was going on, but in retrospect, my denial was kicking in in full force. I soon found myself pregnant with our daughter, and shoved everything

WAY down. In fact, during that time, I would get very angry at anyone that would point out or question any of Joey's issues. "Why is he flapping his hands and arms?" "Why is he jumping like that?" "Why isn't he talking?"

There was a short period of time that I remember him having some strange crying spells. He would suddenly get this blank look on his face and say things like, "Do you see the people?" and some odd phrase that he made up that sounded like, "Sa ba dee". He would say these things while wiggling his fingers in front of his eyes.

I had no idea what he was doing or why he was doing it. He would sit there and cry for no obvious reason with these strange behaviors, and would calm down within a few minutes. I was really scared, but I did not want to admit that anything was wrong with my perfect boy.

So what happened to him?? For my purposes here, suffice it to say that my perfect boy lost an extraordinary amount of language and skills during his second year of life. (including using the potty). My feelings on the subject could fill an entire book on its own. I KNOW he was not born with autism. That is the bottom line.

My Joey is now 13 years old, and we still work every day to gain back all of what he lost back in those early days, and this will continue until I take my last breath.

7. It's my room and I'll eat my walls if I want to…

When Joey was a baby, I always tried to keep his room very cute and practical. As time has gone on however, his room has become an ever changing and evolving work of creativity, mostly for the sake of safety. Apparently, our boy has a strange set of taste buds.

Given the opportunity, he will chew on his walls, curtains, bookcases, closet doors, pillows, blankets, carpets, toys, stuffed animals, mattresses, sheets, clothes, shoes, etc. etc. etc. He wants all of it. Over the last few years, it has become more and more challenging to "camouflage" and cover up his overly tempting vices.

So what's a mama bear to do?? Well, I am always thinking outside the box. Here's just a few examples:

1) His curtains: They are now made from a very durable (but still cute) fabric shower curtain. He can't rip it, it's not stainable, and it's not heavy if it falls down. I put it up with a few fabric tie "loops" that I hang on brackets, so he can open it whenever he wants. I usually have to close it as part of our bedtime routine.

2) The corners of the walls: He just loves to chew on his walls! Years ago, I tried to use those plastic corner protectors around the windows and closet doors to prevent chewing, but he soon snapped them off, and then we were left with jagged and sharp plastic strips (which were much more dangerous than chewing the walls). Then I tried assorted wallpaper borders and the like, but he soon ripped those off as well.

At this point, he has chewed the corners to his satisfaction, and they are no longer tempting to him. This is why they are no longer very attractive either, but I've learned to adapt.

3) Closet doors: Last year, we finally decided to just remove his bi-folding closet doors that he obsessively chewed, and opened up a little "cubby hole" area for him to hang out on his bean bag chair. Very cool.

That opened up "fresh corners" to chew though, so that was the new challenge for a while. I used self-adhesive shelf paper to cover them at first, that worked for some time. He slowly worked his way through that too, however, but the good news is that those corners are no longer tempting to him either. Yay? I don't know. Again, not very attractive.

4) The bookshelf: My husband made this children's bookshelf for me about 20 years ago when I taught preschool. I used it in my classroom for a few years, and then we stored it until we had Joey. Anyway, this is the same bookshelf that he has had in his room since he was born.

A few years ago, he apparently discovered that this thing was DELICIOUS!! Eww. He would chew on it until he needed a smooth spot, and then move over. It was kind of like corn on the cob the way he approached his chewing.

One day, I heard a loud crash, came running upstairs to find him under it. Apparently he was leaning it forward to chew the back. Well, at that point I decided to kill two birds with one stone.

Some weeks earlier, I had put a piece of paneling up on his wall to cover a hole he had made when he was having one of his meltdowns. Well, he had started to pick and chew on the corner of the paneling, which was right next to the bookshelf anyway. So I decided to learn how to use the drill, and screw that darn bookshelf to the wall, right over the corner of the chipping paneling. Voila!! I am quite the decorator!! All to be finished before my hubby came home to see my fancy work, because he rarely approves of my technique. Haha!! All fixed.

5) Beds and mattresses: For most families, I believe that buying mattresses for their children occurs rather infrequently. Obviously, the transition from crib to "big kid" bed is one of them, and then maybe again in the later years of childhood.

Well, this is not the case in our house, at least not for our boy. He is unbelievably hard on his beds. Wowza! Not only does he jump extremely hard and high, but he also has regular "accidents" at night. He will also pick at any thread that he may find until it becomes a large rip. He will slide the mattress half way off of the box spring and then bounce on the middle, causing the entire thing to bend in quite an unnatural fashion.

He can destroy a mattress faster than….well, I don't know, but pretty darn fast. We have to replace his stuff at least every 2 years, and for the second year of that time, we are adding many different covers, protectors, etc. due to the fact that he usually destroys them quite quickly too.

But he sure is good looking!! Hee hee.
I do adore my boy. Love him more than words can say, high maintenance and all.

8. Sibling Love

Ahhh…siblings. Most of us have them, and usually the relationships are complex. Growing up with brothers and sisters helps most of us learn how to navigate relationships. There's usually a lot of drama, arguing, competition, and of course mischief and fun.

Well for my babies, their relationship is a bit different. Joey was three years and four months old when Shayna was born. It was a difficult adjustment for him in the beginning. He was so used to having me to himself, and then he was forced to learn how to share.

Sometimes he would just walk away when I was taking care of the baby, and that would break my heart. He realized pretty quickly, however, that there was enough of me to go around, and that there was plenty of love for him from this new little person too.

The moment I realized just how special their love for each other was, was one day when I had them both in the bathtub. Shayna was just a few months old, and I had her sitting in one of those suction cup thingies facing Joey. I was washing his hair, and I poured a big cup of water over his head. Shayna just TOTALLY CRACKED UP!! It was her first genuine great big belly laugh. She just thought it was hilarious!!

Every time I poured the water on him, she cracked up. Her laughing made Joey and I laugh as well. Such a wonderfully sweet moment. I can't describe how delightfully "normal" it felt. I knew right then and there that their relationship was going to be just fine.

As the years have gone by, Shayna has really become the very best big sister that a little sister ever was. By the time she was two, she already seemed to take on that role. She adores her brother with every fiber of her being.

When she was three, and starting preschool, she stuck an "I love someone with autism" sticker on her folder, and showed it to anyone that would look. By the time she was five, she had a whole bunch of games that she had made up with Joey. Special things that only the two of them could play.

For example, there's "Boinga". She would put her hands under his arms and try to bounce this boy twice her size, all while saying "boinga". So eventually, Joey started asking her for, "Boinga , please" and the rest has followed.

They continue to have all kinds of games like that. The current favorite is "Get your belly", where she sort of softly squeezes his belly and tickles him. When he wants to play he'll say, "I want get your belly please." It's so stinking cute I can hardly even handle it.

Now that they're getting older, she likes to try to teach him all kinds of new things too, not always with much success, but she is very patient and kind. He adores his little sister, and she can almost always make him smile.

Outside of our home life, Shayna has taken an extremely active role in helping me promote autism awareness throughout her school and our town.

Two years ago or so, I asked permission from her PTA to have an "Autism Awareness Week" during the first week of April. They allowed it. So for the past couple years, we have decorated the outside of the school, had the kids wear blue, and changed the marquee sign on the outside of the school to call attention to Autism Awareness Month.

She has spoken on the morning announcements with information about autism each April, and this last year, she, Joey and I even created an informational video that was shown to her entire school!! She is personally responsible for bringing a sense of autism awareness to more than 600 children!! Talk about pride. My goodness she is one amazing sister.

With as many interesting, messy, funny, and even scary scenarios as we have in our home life, she has such a wonderful heart and soul that all she feels for her big brother is the purest love I've ever seen. There is no drama, competition or resentment. She just does what needs to be done, and accepts things the way they are. She has a heart of gold, I tell ya. I am one lucky mama.

9. Home "Improvements"

By no stretch of the imagination have I ever been a clean freak or one of those ultra- organized kind of girls. I was probably right around average or slightly below average in those departments even before my life as a mother.

Little messes didn't bug me, I'd have a stack of papers that I would mean to get to, a pile of laundry sitting somewhere out of place, a few extra dishes in the sink, a bent corner of the blinds that should be replaced, etc. Well, it turns out that this lack of internal obsession for cleaning and organizing is really quite a blessing, or I would be one stressed out mama!!

My life is messy, quite messy, and full of little annoying broken things. Trying to stay on top of all of this is almost impossible. I say "almost" because I have to believe that there may in fact be somebody out there that could keep up with it, unfortunately, that person is not me. Of course, any family of four is capable of creating messes, and causing small bits of damage that require some maintenance,… I know this, don't get me wrong. But mine? Mine most certainly has extra special talents in these departments. For example:

1) The chips!! Omg does Joey love potato chips!! Of course he does. They sure are yummy. But holy moly you would not believe just how messy they can be!! I have chips all over multiple surfaces EVERY SINGLE DAY.

Even when he stays at the table to eat, he drops some on the floor, they get stuck to his clothing, etc. When he stands up, he often steps on a few, that will then stick to his socks, leaving a nice little Hansel and Gretel trail behind him as he goes on his way. Now many times, he will also sneak an extra handful before getting up, walking and crunching and dropping extra crumbs as he goes. It's loads of fun to watch. Ugh.

2) The walls!! My boy has a strange habit of touching the walls as he walks around. Well, that probably wouldn't be a problem if he didn't do it right after eating!! Sheesh.

3) Red plastic cups: We can't use glass drinking glasses in our house for obvious reasons, and the hard plastic ones are too hard and heavy for when Joey does his 'tapping" and banging thing that he likes to do with cups. He enjoys making up rhythms, but the hard cups are not safe if he should decide to bang on a window, so we started using the disposable red plastic cups.

He is now completely obsessed with them. It started with this crazy ability he had to mimic my husband's "on call" ring from his work phone, with a certain way he would shake the red cup. It was so weird. Spot on.

Then for some reason, he started to "crack" the cups in a certain spot, and peel them into strips. He then plays with each strip, shaking them, bending them, chewing them, etc. So now I have the pleasure of finding pieces of red plastic cups strewn throughout the house, particularly the mother- load (pun fully intended) of little strips that I periodically find in his bedroom. Oh the joy of it all.

4) Blinds and window coverings: Because of his love for strings, strips, and pretty much anything long and pliable, we have to be careful with blinds and curtains in our house.

We have old vertical blinds in the kitchen and family room. They may be old and ugly, but on the plus side, it doesn't bother me when he plays with the cord or bends one of the panels. I know how to pop in a vertical blind panel like nobody's business. I've even learned that once one side is worn out from popping it in and out too much, you can flip them upside down and use the other side!! Yay!!

Then there's the living room blinds. We recently had to replace those because my boy had pretty much destroyed them. They were made of a paper thin material in a pleated blind with no strings. It was great until I found that he had ripped huge holes in them one day when I wasn't looking. I actually used scotch tape to fix them a couple of times (more of my "technique" that my husband loves so much) but to no avail.

So Shayna and I headed off to Home Depot in search of some "Joey proof" window coverings. The saleslady was very nice, showing us this and that, as Shayna and I were discussing the potential problems with each one. "He'll definitely eat this one." "He'll peel this one apart for sure." "This one is too heavy if it falls on his head"… and so on.

When I looked up and saw the puzzled look on the poor saleswoman's face, I totally cracked up. I can't even imagine the crazy house she was envisioning!! I told her a little bit about Joey at that point, and we all giggled a little at the craziness of the whole thing. We ended up just buying a new version of our old blinds. Never a dull moment!!

10. Go to Sleep!!

In the autism world, I know my son would be considered a pretty good sleeper... in the reality of my world, however, that is not, and has not, always been the case. Nightly melatonin has been extremely helpful in regulating Joey's sleep cycle, but we still have our rough patches.

When he was younger, he would take FOREVER to calm down in his room at bedtime. He would bounce, sing, jump, bang etc., every night, for at least an hour or two. He would come out of his room and wander around, and I would put him back to bed. This would happen over and over again, as he and I both became more and more exhausted.

Sometimes he would finally fall asleep, just to wake up in a few hours and start the whole process all over again. I have always been strict with bedtimes, but you can only lead a horse to water, ya know what I mean? As the years have gone by, he has gotten much better about staying in his room when he wakes up, but if he's awake, I'm awake. That's what Mama ears are for, right?

There is one particular occasion that comes to mind. One night a few years ago, I got to sneak out of my house after everyone was FINALLY asleep and go to a neighbor's house for a few Mama cocktails. (Leaving the sleeping hubby who is not equipped with Mama ears home with the kiddos). It was the night before the Fourth of July, and I wanted to partake in some of the fun I was hearing outside, so I ventured out.

I didn't get home until 4:00am!! Can you guess what happened next? Of course !! My beautiful boy woke up and started singing and giggling right when I walked into my bedroom to go to sleep!! I was so exhausted, and a little tipsy...and the best part of the whole thing was that I had promised my daughter that for the first time, I would take her and Joey to the Fourth of July parade in town at 9:00 am the next morning.

I can still remember my slightly drunken state of disbelief and panic in that moment. Wowza. I know I didn't sleep much that night, but I did indeed get up and take them both to the parade in the morning, with a pretty nice headache in tow.

I don't know if every town does this, but apparently my town has an extremely fond affection for using emergency vehicles, and their respective horns and sirens as part of their parade festivities. OMG. Not only was my head pounding, but Joey HATES those kinds of loud noises!! It was a nightmare.

Oh...and did I mention that while Joey was freaking out because of the noise, the vehicles in the parade were throwing candy into the street so my little daughter, who was around 5 at the time, was running in front of moving vehicles to try to get candy??? Oh yeah, and by the way, I was by myself with both kids, lawn chairs, and no way to leave because of the parade traffic. Good times!! Ha!!

It's kind of funny now I guess, but that experience was just one of many that have earned me my autism mama stripes. Ugh.

11. Peace and Quiet?

Ha! Nope.

12. I want music please...

Joey responds unbelievably well to music...I would even have to say that rock-n-roll is his preferred language. Myself, my husband and our daughter (who is the best "big sister" that a little sister ever was!!) make up our own lyrics to new and classic rock songs for just about every activity in this kid's day!

For example, we might sing "Rock-n-Roll All Night" by KISS as, "I'm...gonna take a bath tonight....and brush my teeth every day!" He will fill in the blanks when we sing...where with spoken words, we don't usually get much of a response.

He loves great music from The Beatles, to Johnny Cash, to The Who, and everything in between. I sometimes wonder what we must sound like to other motorists on the road, as we drive along belting out our favorite tunes.

Music helps all of us become part of the same world. Our little family was brought together by a love of rock-n-roll, and continues to grow in that love year after year. It gives us an outlet, while allowing us to remain at least partially sane.

Together , with a little help from the rock gods, we can roll through whatever it is that life throws our way.

13. How do we hear each other's brains? Seriously?

Since day one, and probably well before, I have had an amazingly strong connection and bond with my beautiful boy. I can't really explain it in words, but we have what feels like a pathway of sorts between our two brains. I understand that this may sound crazy, but that doesn't make it any less true.

Many times this kid can actually hear what I'm thinking!! It goes the other way too, but I wish I could do it as well as he

can. Here's just a few examples to help you understand what I'm saying:

When Joey was a baby, about 1 or so, I was changing him on the changing table in his room. I wasn't saying anything at the moment, I was just thinking that maybe I would take him to my mom's house that day. I said NOTHING out loud. At that exact moment, this kid looked up at me and said, "Grammy". It blew my mind!! SO weird.

There was another time when he was two. I was such a freak about leaving him at this "terrific twos" one hour , once a week, park district class. (I know you're shocked that I didn't want to leave him...haha) I didn't like it that I couldn't watch.

The only windows were way up above the doors, and yes, I did consider climbing on tables and chairs to see, but I restrained myself. My husband suggested that I get a periscope. I think he was joking, but I would have bought one had I known where to get it.

Anyway, because I couldn't watch him, I would always hang out and listen from the hallway. One day during class, I tried peeking through the tiniest little crack of a door jam, trying to get a look at my baby, but I could only see one tiny little spot of the fairly large room.

Well, guess who came directly to that spot and plopped himself down?? My Joey!! Yay!! He could absolutely feel me there. This kind of thing has happened several more times over the years during school observations and the like as well. Sometimes even through a two way mirror!! So funny!!

To this day, if I am in my bedroom or something, and decide that I might want to go downstairs to get a cookie, it would not be unusual for this kid to come in my room and say, "cookie please". Weird stuff like that happens all the time.

Now from my side, hearing his brain, I am the best guess going when it comes to figuring out my kid. He cannot verbally or even gesturally express what is hurting him, or why he's frustrated or mad or sad, etc. etc. etc. His language is pretty much limited to requesting highly desirable items and activities.

Somehow, however, most of the time, I know what he is wanting, thinking and feeling. At least I think I'm usually pretty close. Man, I love that kid.

14. The Gluten Free / Casein Free Diet Adventure…(GF/CF)

"The Diet". Hmmm. OK…Joey was gluten and casein free for about a year and a half, starting when he was 5, and ending when he was about 6 and a half. The GF/CF diet loosely defined, basically means that your child may not eat ANY wheat or dairy products, in any amount or form, at ANY time.   It is an extremely tough diet to follow, but of course if it would have helped him, we would have done it forever.

Back in those days, GF/CF products were not readily available in your neighborhood grocery store. Only specialty stores carried most of the products, and everything was very expensive. I was spending several hundred dollars a month on his food alone. It was quite financially draining.

I have heard many wonderful success stories from families that swear by the diet, and I may try it again at some point, but I guess I am a little bit gun shy.

What makes it a little extra tricky is that Joey is the most verbal about food, and he LOVES to eat. I don't know how likely it would be for him to have success with it now, versus when he was younger, but I try not to rule anything out.

When he was on the diet, I had to keep all foods for the house separated. He even had his own toaster and dishes. "Experts" say that one crumb of gluten could be enough to spark a reaction in these sensitive kids. There are all kinds of biological reasons that these kids can't tolerate gluten. So when you are spending tons of money, energy, and other resources on a spearheaded effort to help improve your child's health, and something really stupid comes along to screw it up...it's almost unbearable!

For example: When you are taking your GF/CF child with you to an autism conference of all things, and you stop at a particular fast food restaurant that specifically says that they have gluten free french fries, order them, blow on them to make sure they are not too hot, hand them to your GF/CF six year old in the back seat, and look up in your rear view mirror to find a great big BREADED ONION RING hanging out of his mouth!!! I still get SOOOOO furious when I think about that moment. Although I did get $1500 bucks out of them completely on my own. Don't mess with this Mama bear's cub. Grrrr.

15. Boing! Boing! Boing!

When we named our son "Joey", we had no idea that he would completely share the same instinct and passion for jumping as his namesake, the baby kangaroo. My boy is a JUMPER!! He jumps and bounces around like nobody's business.

Not only does he love to bounce on beds, trampolines and bouncy houses, but this kid can have a bounce in his step no matter where he is! He will suddenly jump 5, 10, or even 20 times in a row, just standing on a regular floor.

Since he has done this for so many years, I am quite used to it, but since he is a lot bigger now, I can't say the same thing for our poor floors!! When he jumps in his room, which is on the second floor, you can feel the vibrations and hear the noise throughout the rest of the house. He will jump when he's overly excited or happy, but he will also go into an extra loud stomping kind of jump when he is on the verge of a meltdown

(I'll go into that a little more in another section).

The most memorable jumping episode in recent history was a couple years ago, when my mom and I took the kids to a free museum in Kenosha, WI. It was a fun day. We started with a picnic lunch outside, and then went into the museum to look around.

Well, we got to this one exhibit that had several historic artifacts, all enclosed in cases. Seemed Joey proof enough…but I guess not exactly. We were walking through one of the exhibits, when Joey went into one of his jumping crazes.

There was a vase in a large case right in front of us, that actually started to do the death wobble. My mom and I just looked at each other in sheer shock and panic, as we watched this vase wobble and spin, wobble and spin, wobble and spin, and then finally stop…miraculously staying in its upright position. Holy heart attack!!! That was nuts!!

We laughed so hard as we quickly hightailed our way out of that exhibit. It was definitely a different kind of museum visiting experience. A day that may or may not have been very memorable, now has images that are forever burned into our brains. Pretty funny though, since it all worked out okay, but sheesh…

16. Meltdowns…

Oh yes, the severely dreaded , nerve fraying, heartbreaking, stomach wrenching, highly feared, massive meltdowns. Hmmm. The nucleus of all that can go south very quickly in virtually any scenario in my life with my boy. Sometimes I can see them coming, and sometimes I can't.

As the years have gone by, and he has become bigger and stronger, these episodes have gotten much more intense. Looking back, I don't remember Joey having meltdowns as a very little guy. I think he was already 5 or so when he first starting showing a few signs of aggression toward some of his teachers at school. (Only during those "episodes"...otherwise he was his sweet, smiley, and happy self).

At that point, I had never experienced this at home, but he had started pinching and scratching his teachers when he would become frustrated or agitated. I slowly started to see these behaviors at home as well, but only during times that demands were being placed on him (such as doing a puzzle, matching, coloring, etc.).

As time went on, however, both his school and myself started noticing these behaviors at what seemed to be spontaneous and/or unpredictable times as well. I started to refer to this as the unknown "x factor" in Joey. Obviously I knew that something had to be bothering him, but he wasn't able to tell me what it was (and he still can't).

Thankfully, much of the time I am a pretty good guesser as to what might be bothering him, but even then, sometimes either I don't catch it in time, or it's something that I cannot see or hear, such as a tummy ache, headache, stubbed toe, tooth ache, or maybe even a little hang nail. I think that when there is not an obvious trigger, his "x factor" is usually in the form of some sort of physical discomfort that he cannot express.

I can't even imagine how horribly scary and frustrating those moments are for him. I think that any one of us would likely have a huge meltdown if we were in his shoes. Anyway, I have learned how to react quite quickly when I see his frustration beginning to escalate.

Up until about a year ago, it was somewhat easier to handle him on my own when he would get into one of his aggressive states. It's a lot harder for me to handle him now. He can get pretty aggressive.

There is no reasoning or even bribing this kid once he reaches a certain level. He has, "left the building" so to speak. I could ask him if he wants to eat donuts while he jumps into the pool from the trampoline and he would not even hear me.

I wish I could say that these tantrums were a rare

occurrence, but unfortunately, they are not. There are times when he goes weeks without any issues, but then he may have days or even weeks where he has one every few hours.

There is no doubt that this is our biggest autism hurdle. I have had to make many extremely quick, non-graceful getaways from all sorts of venues, events, and situations. One time we had to leave the movie theater so fast that we actually left his shoes inside!! It was not summer!!

But even in those moments, those awful, stressful, sad and horrible moments, sometimes a stranger's kindness can make all the difference in the world. After I had Joey safely belted into the car in the theater parking lot, a nice lady that had been sitting near us in the movie walked up to me, gave me a hug, and handed me Joey's shoes. She told me that she thought I was a great mom, and went on her way. It was really nice to hear that at that particular moment. Her kind words mixed a few happy tears in with my sad ones. Timing can be everything.

As I write this, I am currently working with Joey's neurologist to see if there are any medications that might be able to help him. It's just so hard because I don't trust any of the drug companies, and I don't want to cause additional problems such as horrible side effects or drastic personality changes in my sweet baby. I can't count on anyone else to "protect" him. That's my job. I do hope, however, that someday very soon, I can be more confident in the choices that I make.

I would love to just take him everywhere without always having to have a "getaway plan". I would love to know that he is calm and comfortable and feeling great. I don't think that this is unattainable, at this point though, it's still very much a work in progress.

17. Shhhhhhh...

Somehow, over the years, I have become the official "shoosher" in my house. It's a crappy job, but somebody has to do it.

Joey is highly sensitive to certain loud tones, voices, and noises, and hearing them when he is not in the right mood can easily result in a huge meltdown. For this reason, as I try to keep the undesirable noises in my house to a minimum, I have had to take on the role of "shoosh enforcer".

Nobody likes it, and I don't like it either, but it's better than the alternative. Now why I seem to be the only one in my house (be it resident or visitor) that is actually aware of the noises that bother Joey, I am not sure. You would think that maybe the others might have caught on by this point, but unfortunately, they haven't. Well, maybe they are aware, but it seems that until I "shoosh" them, their noisy antics will go unchanged.

In their defense, I too never truly realized how loud normal daily life activities can be until Joey became so sensitive. The fact remains, however, that he IS that sensitive, and we all need to adjust. Maybe it's not, "fair", that we have to keep it down sometimes, but it is what it is, and getting irritated with me most certainly won't help solve the problem.

He does wear sound blocking headphones, but they only help to a certain point, and he doesn't always have them on at the right moment. I do SOOO wish that he could just tell everybody to shut the heck up instead of getting so upset, but he can't. So as the mama bear, keeping the noise level down within his comfort level has become my job.

18. You can't fool me, mister!!

Daily life around here can be slightly chaotic to say the least. There are many things that Joey cannot yet do for himself, so as the mama, I absorb much of what needs to be done to help him, into my own daily routines.

It's funny though, while he may often seem like he's not catching on, he also appears to be quite capable of using complex skills when he sees fit. I have come to understand that sometimes he needs to be extremely highly motivated to make things happen.

With my sweet boy, sometimes his motivation comes from knowing that something is important to me. As with much in my life, these small acts of independence often catch me by surprise. For example, I am kind of crazy, fanatical, nutso about closing the sliding screen door to the backyard in the summertime, and we are in and out A LOT. I hate when the bugs get in the house, it drives me nuts.

Well, I'll be darned if my mysterious, sometimes seemingly oblivious, beautiful, smart, wonderfully amazing boy doesn't close that screen door behind him almost every time he goes in and out of the house. It makes me wonder what he might be capable of if I was obsessive compulsive about everything else in his life!!

Would he read if I insisted that everybody read before they eat? Would he use the bathroom if I made everybody go before listening to music or watching The Wiggles? I don't know! But I can't seem to make myself obsess in an effective way to zero in on his other potential skills!!

This independence thing can also come out in the form of sneakiness as well. He will absolutely wait until I am not paying attention to get into mischief. If he puts something in his mouth that he shouldn't, he will spit it out when I look at him. I don't even say a word, sometimes I don't even know he has anything in his mouth!

Then there was that time few years ago when he was still on the GF/CF diet, and he sneaked into the pantry, found and opened a hidden package of regular chocolate chip cookies, stole a bunch of them, and ate them completely unnoticed while I was just a few feet away in the other room.

Now I don't know about you, but at my current age, with my own sneaking abilities, there is no way in the world that I could open a noisy package of "Chips Ahoy" without everybody knowing about it. It was like for that moment, he had the hands of a surgeon. I just never know what that kid might be capable of. Never a dull moment!!

19. Really, honey? You'll eat leaves and dirt, but my dinner makes you gag?

Oh my silly boy...always a puzzle. Yep, there is not much more humbling than presenting your child (that will pretty much put anything in his mouth) with a nice home cooked meal, just to have him either smell it and push it away, or put it to his lips and actually gag. It happens every so often, and never fails to make me re-evaluate my culinary skills.

He actually threw up one time when I gave him a bite of my homemade chicken soup. He really did!! I may not have been quite as stunned, if he hadn't still had a slightly visible ring of dirt around his mouth from playing outside right before dinner. Hmmm.

20. Our first house: The pool, the tick, and the lottery...

Yes, my husband and I were together for almost 10 years before getting married, but we didn't purchase our first home until after the wedding, when I became pregnant with Joey.

We decided on a townhouse that we could afford on only his income (actually we were going to be broke as hell once I stopped working, so in retrospect, I use the term "afford" quite loosely). We would live there for almost 5 years.

Joey was born in December of 2000, and by June, we had him in the complex pool which was right outside of our house. He LOVED it!! I am a fish, and so is my husband, so the fact that Joey loved the water came as no surprise to us. What was a surprise, however, was that every single time I brought that baby in the water, he would spit up.

No biggie when he was 6 months old. This continued every summer as he got older though, so then it kind of became a problem. (We had the same lifeguard every year). He would always put his face in, swallow water, cough, choke, and puke. Particularly troublesome on days that he had had Cheetos with his lunch.

Now on the plus side of this gross problem, I did create an

amazing bond and friendship with a wonderful neighbor and her family. They lived near the pool as well. Her youngest daughter and Joey are only one week apart.

We became fast friends, and together, would even try to hide Joey's puking from the lifeguard. At least we had gotten pretty good at getting him to the side of the pool in time. Eventually, I did get a baby pool and sprinkler to supplement our time in the big pool, this made the lifeguard happy. It was kind of a stress reliever for me too. It gave us mamas some time to play, without having to be in the water with the kids every second. We had a lot of great times. We would hang out during the rest of the year too, and they were the best neighbors ever.

Late one spring, Darin and I took our kids to Springfield, IL for a weekend of touristy fun. We had saved up a little money to take a weekend trip, and were treating ourselves to a little family getaway.

By this point, Shayna was about a year old and Joey was about 4 and a half. I still had panic attack issues, but I had accepted that my sweet boy did indeed have some form of autism, and he was scheduled to start in an autism preschool program in the fall.

The weekend was fun in a typical Mitchell crazy kind of way. Shayna had a fever, it rained a lot, and we did everything that we wanted to do in spite of the hurdles (Thank goodness for baby Tylenol). We really did have a good time.

The last morning, as we were heading back to our room from the hotel breakfast, my husband suddenly stopped cold and said in a scary voice, "What is THAT on Joey's head?" Then he proceeded to tell me that it was a TICK!!! A great big tick that had apparently been feasting on our boy's head since our picnic at the woods about a week earlier!! OMG. Anyway, he got it out, we flushed it, and went on our way home.

Once home, I did a better check of Joey's thick dark haired head, only to discover ANOTHER tick!!! By this time, I was totally freaking out!! I had Darin shave Joey's head with the clippers (which he did WAY shorter than I meant ,and the child was almost bald). But at least it was clear that there were no more ticks. I decided I would take him to the doctor in the morning to make sure he was OK.

As I'm sitting on my front step, processing all that had transpired over this crazy weekend, my favorite neighbor in the world comes over and plops down next to me. She's smiling kind of a funny smile, so I asked her what was up. She looks at me and says, "Did you hear about that local family that won the lottery?" I looked at her blankly and said no. She pointed to herself with a big old grin, and I was just floored.

Turned out that while I was trying to have a fun weekend, getting rained on with a sick baby, and picking ticks out of my autistic son's head, my favorite family in the world had just won 5 million dollars in the lottery. WOW. No words. Every emotion.

Let's just say I was not impressed with God's sense of humor at that moment. It was a process, but I did accept the situation as it was, and of course I was happy for my dear friends. I had to go through some serious soul searching that night though. Sheesh.

Anyway, that was about 8 or 9 years ago. Since then, they moved, we moved, we're still friends, and we still hang out on occasion. We live 12 minutes from driveway to driveway. It's all good. Much, much, much love. You just never know what life has in store for us!! Once again, always an adventure!!

**PLEASE NOTE: I very rarely use the word "autistic". I don't like it, and it makes me cringe. Yes, my Joey has autism, but that is by no means ALL that he is. I struggled to come up with a different word to effectively convey my feelings at that moment in time, but to no avail. Ok…I feel better now. Carry on.

21. Holy Laundry, Batman!!

My son is quite possibly one of the messiest human beings on the planet. I say this with love, but nonetheless, it is still very true. He goes through clean clothes, sheets, blankets, etc. faster than I can possibly hope to keep up. I have often said that I need a tissue box style of clothing and bedding for him, so when one gets dirty, I can just pop the next one right out of the box.

I still help him to dress, and I am also the one that makes up his bed, so since last time I checked, I still have a body, bed, and clothing of my own, plus my daughter and my lovely, ever so sparkling clean plumber husband, who thankfully does his own laundry, but is often in my way with his load consisting of two shirts, a pair of pants, and a pair of underwear and socks. Seriously?? My loads weigh about 10,000 pounds, and I will still need to do more when it's done.

In fact, as I write this, our dryer is not working, so I am literally hanging all of our laundry to dry. It sucks!!! I feel like a pioneer woman on The Oregon Trail, only I am pretty darn sure that her children's laundry wasn't even as dirty as Joey's. He's pretty rough on his clothes too. Some shirts have little holes from chewing, or a loose string that was pulled too far, or a stain that I couldn't get out. I joke that even if I won the lottery and could buy him new clothes every day, the clothes that he only wore once would STILL probably not be accepted by Goodwill.

Anyway, an average day pretty much goes like this...I get my boy up and out of bed, his P.J.'s are almost always wet. He wears a pull up, but apparently things go a little crazy in there during the night, so the sheets and blankets get a bit wet fairly regularly as well. I have recently started taking off the dirty jammies in the morning, and then waiting until AFTER breakfast to put on his clean clothes. This probably saves me a few dirty outfits per week (I'll take what I can get). OK, so it's not even 7:30am and I already have potentially dirty jammies, sheets, blankets, and "breakfast clothes" if it's a cold morning.

Moving on...we get dressed, brush the teeth, brush the hair, wash the face, sparkling clean and ready for school. He has a long ride (an hour and 15 minutes with no traffic, but I'll get into that later), so I'm pretty sure by the time he arrives at school, he only has cracker crumbs, apple stickiness, and water on himself from the snack I give him for the ride.

School clothes also feed the laundry pile. I send in extra clothes, but undoubtedly, every so often he will come home with "borrowed" clothes that belong to the school. I am not proud of this, but unfortunately I have become one of "those parents" that does not promptly return these borrowed clothes. I mean to, but somehow they get caught up in the laundry craziness in my house, and eventually, I just send him back to school wearing them.

When he gets home from school, about fifty percent of the time he needs to change clothes when he gets in the house. Once settled in, there is usually at least one more change of clothes before his jammies go on at bedtime. Rinse, lather, repeat. Rinse, lather, repeat. I am not doing the math here, but HOLY LAUNDRY, BATMAN!!

22. Our Boy Should Really Be a Product Tester...

There are not many things in this world that are completely "Joey Proof". He has his own unique way of destroying things...it is almost an art form. Between his desire for bouncing, chewing, picking, peeling, tapping, ripping, tasting, flipping, flapping, shaking, etc., I have to tell you, I see the world with a different set of eyes than most parents.

When we are out and about, there is no object too big or too small for Joey to "test". SOOO why not put this amazing talent to good use? Maybe we can start with, "mattress tester"???

23. The Pool, the Noodles, and the Baby Ruth...

Living in the Midwest, there is nothing more exciting weather wise than the end of winter. We are always so anxious for spring, and that moment sometime in late May when we can begin to open up the pool.

That day is often one of mixed emotions for my Joey. He starts off with HUGE smiles, but usually seems to forget that setting up the pool is a process, and we can't just jump in and swim on the first day. Sometimes he will even go find last year's sunscreen in the cabinet, hand it to me, and say "Lotion please." Such an innocent little sweet heart. Love him.

Anyway, his initial reaction always reminds me of that scene in National Lampoon's Vacation, when The Griswolds finally arrive at Wally World. They run in slow motion to the theme music from Chariots of Fire, with all of this joy, excitement and enthusiasm, just to get to the entrance, and hear that stupid moose tell them that Wally World is closed for repairs. Poor Joe…but over the next few days, the chemicals do their thing, the water warms up, and we are finally good to go.

We all love the pool, but my Joey…he LOOOOVVVVESSSS it the most!!! During the summer at our house, he and I are rarely indoors. He has so much fun in the water, that people can probably hear him splashing, laughing and carrying on from a mile away. And holy cow, the pool noodles!! This kid makes noises with a noodle that can probably be heard from the moon. He whacks those things so incredibly hard on the water's surface, that if you didn't know better, you might think we were lighting off fireworks in our yard. Thankfully, my neighbors don't seem to mind, and if they do, they are nice enough to pretend that they don't.

Now the pottying issue has long been somewhat of a problem with swimming (On the plus side, though, he no longer pukes in the pool!!). I have tried a lot of different swimsuits, pull ups, shorts, pants, etc. over the years to try and solve this problem, but once again, as with many products, finding one that works for Joey has proven to be quite a challenge).

At this point though, I have gotten pretty good at either preventing the issue altogether by strategically planning when to keep him out of the water, and/or by watching for his

"warning sign" while he swims. (aka his "pooping face").
Thankfully he does listen when I tell him to get out, and I
think we only had one accident this last summer. I also keep a
lot of extra chlorine and a good pool vacuum on hand just in
case. Yep...I am one persistent mama. Nothing's gonna stop
me from letting my boy enjoy his beloved pool!! Nothing!!

24. SOOOOO Busted!! The Basement, Daddy's Paint, and The Man Cave...

When we chose our house, one of the requirements was
that it have a basement to house the "Man Cave". It didn't
need to be finished, it just needed to serve as a hang
out/recording studio/art studio/hiding place for my dear
sweet husband (said "mostly" with love, but why every
human being in my house, excluding only myself, seems to be
entitled to their very own private space, is kind of a bum deal
for me, especially considering the fact that I can't even go to
the bathroom to pee without somebody needing my
IMMEDIATE attention).

But anyhow, one Saturday afternoon ,after being in our
house about a year, our then, 5 year old Joey had apparently
sneaked down into the basement when nobody was looking.
How do I know this? Well, because as I walked around the
corner, into my kitchen that fateful afternoon, near the
basement door, there stood a little boy with a goofy smile,
covered from head to toe in BLACK PAINT!!! Thank goodness
it wasn't red or I may have had a heart attack right then and
there.

As my hubby and I followed the trail of black goop down

the basement stairs, it lead us straight to a tube of black acrylic paint that had been removed from my husband's painting easel. Following the trail a bit further revealed hand and footprints all over the rugs, couches, and walls of the finely decorated and highly prized, "man cave" Holy moly!! Not only was that paint impossible to get off of the assorted surfaces in the basement, (he lived with the hand prints for a while but has since replaced the "furnishings")…but it was also quite a project to get that black gunk off of a little five year old boy. Ugh.

At least I think we scared the crap out of him though, because he hasn't tried to sneak down into the basement alone since, and this happened about 7 years ago!! Craziness!!

25. "Me Time"???...Pfffft...

Roses are red.
Violets are blue.
When you are a mama bear…
There's not much time for you.
The End.

26. "Alone Time" for Mama & Daddy (The couple formerly known as Darin & Suz)

To put it mildly, we don't get out much. I don't even remember the last time we went out to dinner together, (just the two of us) much less a romantic night or two away. I think it was about 9 years ago when the two of us last stayed away overnight, and I was still having panic attacks over Joey at the time. (Yes, VERY romantic!)

It's so hard for us to go out (with the kids is way hard too, but for now, I'm only talking about grown up time). Between the stress of a possible meltdown when my parents come to babysit, and the extra money that we don't really have or want to spend, it's almost an impossible feat. If we wait until Joey goes to bed, we can sometimes have my parents come so we can sneak out to a party in our neighborhood, but besides that, we are pretty much either home, or out with the kids.

So why??? I know that our relationship suffers for it. I know that we don't have enough fun together. It's just that the amount of preparation and planning that it takes ME to set things up for an evening of "fun" is so stressful. I have to think of every possible scenario that could arise when I am not there…not only because I'm crazy, but because there are real and genuine dangers that exist for everyone involved if I don't.

Going through this process of, "getting ready", also seems to set me up for resenting my husband, who does not understand how hard it is for me get to get all of these things in order, and then "relax". He gets stressed out and irritated with me because I am doing what I need to do before we go, I get mad at him because he doesn't understand or appreciate the fact that I am attempting to achieve the impossible just to have some fun "alone time" with him, and then we fight. It's just a vicious cycle.

So if at this lovely point we are lucky enough to get out of the house, unless I know Joey is asleep, I am now pretending to relax, but actually worrying about what's going on at home. OK, maybe I'm a little crazy, but I know my kid, and like I've said a million times, I can't explain him in a nutshell.

SOOO…If we could always wait until Joey's asleep, then maybe we could go out more often to have some fun?? Well, that sounds great, but with the life we lead, we are REALLY tired by the end of the day, and we want to go to bed too!! Thankfully there are some after dark, "home activities" that we still very much enjoy doing together. Tee hee.

27. Straw Thief...

When Joey was a little baby, I used to drip a small amount of water, juice, etc. into his mouth using a straw. I would put my finger on the end, and release the little bit of liquid into his mouth. He loved it. Well, apparently his love for straws is one that is here to stay, only now, he is OBSESSED with them!! He doesn't really seem to care if he drinks out of it, he just wants to play with it. Bending, shaking, chewing, tapping, etc.

Oh…the best one is when it's a straw that is fresh out of a drink, and he shakes the little droplets all over the place. This is particularly pleasant when we are in public, and people look up to see what is dripping on them. Oy.

Anyway, I cannot have a straw sitting in my drink, at any time without Joey wanting it. He will plot his attack very carefully, and then wait until I look away to snatch it. When I buy a new package of straws for the house, I have to hide them. This kid gets more excited to steal mass quantities of straws than he does to steal cookies. I'm serious... and this boy LOVES his cookies!! He's such a goof ball.

28. Headphones Make Me Happy...

I think Joey was 6 or 7 when he first came home from school wearing a pair of sound blocking/noise reduction headphones. They are the type that a construction worker or a hunter might wear; they do not play music, but are strictly designed to reduce noise.

What a difference!! Holy Moly!! He was suddenly able to ride in the car with his sister without getting mad. He was able to sit in a restaurant without that same huge level of anxiety. He no longer kept his fingers in his ears, so his hands were free to do other things. This is a kid that would never leave a hat on his head for 2 seconds, but he learned very quickly that these headphones made him happy, and he still puts them on all the time. Hands down, (pun fully intended) the single biggest lifestyle changer for our boy...EVER!!

In the last few years, however, Joey has started to "reconfigure" his headphones every time I buy him a new pair. Unfortunately, when he does this, it makes them somewhat less effective, causing some of his sensitivities to certain noises to return. Here's kind of how the situation has evolved...He had his first pair of headphones for a few years with no issues. One day a couple years ago, he ripped off the padded covers, pulled out the foam, and chewed up much of the plastic. I thought for sure it was just because they were old and not comfortable anymore, so I ordered new ones.

Well, they came, and he destroyed the new pair on the first day. Ugh. Hmmm. His school gave him the next pair, and once again, he ripped them apart. I ordered them one or two more times, to have them suffer the same fate, and then finally realized that he wanted them that way.

So now, he wears his own "Joey styled" custom headphones, that are not nearly as effective as they could and should be for his sensitivity to certain noises, but apparently, they are exactly the way he wants them. Hmmm.

29. "I Love...I Love You"/ One Happy Mama

I have always told my kids how much I love them at least a few times a day, every single day, since they were born...in fact even when they were in utero. Normally, I can get Joey to say it back once in a while, but only when I say it first, and only after I make an obvious face like I'm waiting for him to say it back... then he'll say the rehearsed, "I love you too, Mama" which I'll take any way I can get!!

But...ON THIS DAY, my Joey came up to snuggle with me on the couch, wrapped his arms around my neck and said, completely out of nowhere..."I love, I love you." Wow, wow, wow!!!!! I cried happy tears for like a half hour, while Joey just kept smiling with awesome snuggles and giggles, loving how happy he made me. When he walked away, and I ran to tell Darin and Shayna, I even had the ugly cry for a few minutes. Haha. Man I love that kid!!

30. I Wish I Had Done Better in biology...

Quite frankly, I have never been a science minded person. I was always a fairly good student, but science was never one of my best subjects. The thing is, it's not that I didn't try, my mind is just not wired that way.

Well, that was a fine slap into reality when I was tossed into the world of autism, gut issues, and biomedical treatments. Not to mention the pharmaceutical end of things. Holy cow. It's frustrating because I know there are potentially life-changing treatments out there for my boy, but it's all so freakin' complicated... not to mention excruciatingly expensive, and of course, NOT covered by insurance.

We have tried many things, and there are still many left to try...but sadly, and quite inexcusably if you ask me, there are STILL not enough reliable resources out there to help all of our families navigate and utilize these extremely scary, outrageously expensive, and ridiculously and unnecessarily controversial treatments.

Why do we all have to start from scratch?? It's such a lonely and treacherous path for so many of us. It shouldn't have to be that way, but it is. The numbers keep going up, "awareness" seems to be more prevalent, yet services are still WAYYY behind the times. Something truly monumental has to happen very soon....It just has to. If only it wasn't so messy. Big sigh...

31. Just a Random Funny...

Just a funny thing to share...I took the kids to see a $1 movie during the summer. Well, when I looked over at my boy, he had his mouth wide open, and the almost empty popcorn bucket covering most of his head!! Really, Joe?? Haha!! It was a sad part of the movie too, so suddenly I was the inappropriate one...laughing way too loud. Always an adventure... :-))

32. "Do I want to teach special ed.? Nahhh."...

When I started college, I wanted to be in advertising, but I had a crappy teacher for my first experience, and that was the end of that. It's a bummer because I still think I would be great in that field. Anyway, I decided to major in Psychology, picturing myself going on to get my PhD, and opening my own office.

Well, I earned my bachelor's in Psychology, but then decided that I wanted to be a teacher. Ahh...the decisions of youth. Like I said earlier, I ALWAYS knew that I would someday be home with my babies. I figured that teaching would at least give me the option to go back to work when they got older, while still having early hours, days off, and summers with my at that point, still "imaginary" kids. I would still be able to help people, just in a classroom setting instead of an office.

Yep...I had a plan, Stan. So off to graduate school I went. I found a college with a graduate program that combined both, teaching credentials and a Master's Degree. I was able to take evening classes and still keep my job as a preschool teacher.

Then I had a choice to make... special education, or not? Hmm. The funny thing is... it was a pretty easy decision. I did not think that I had that certain quality necessary to work with "special needs" children. My passion, I thought, was for the mainstream world of education. HA!! God's crazy sense of humor at work again I suppose.

SOOO, I earned my master's degree, became a certified teacher, and started looking for a job. By this time, I was 26, and Darin and I had just gotten married. I soon came to realize that elementary school teaching jobs were in very high demand, and regular education teachers were pretty much a dime a dozen. Yay.

So, I signed up to become a substitute. Within several months, I landed a "maternity leave" position in a great school district, and was quite likely a "shoo- in" for a full time position the following year (the teacher I was covering for had decided not to return). A couple months later, I found out I was pregnant with my Joey. We had just started "trying", but you hear all kinds of stories about people taking a long time to get pregnant...apparently not us. Ha ha.

I was home with my babies for the next seven years or so...until Shayna started preschool. Between our regular expenses and our numerous autism expenses, I had to earn some money somehow. So since I knew my life would not allow me to fully commit to a classroom, and both kids were in school for at least part of the day, I started to sub again. (Not nearly enough money, but at least I was able to take days off whenever I needed, no grading, homework, etc.)

By that time, I realized that "special ed" was indeed something that I was passionate about, and I have actually been subbing for the Special Ed District in our county ever since. The irony of that is, I didn't start working for them until AFTER we hired lawyers, screamed and yelled, and fought tooth and nail to pull Joey out of their program, and get our district to pay for his private placement…Funny huh? We won by the way. More on that later.

33. I Must Get My Hands on that Cream!!

Autism has a way of bringing out my strongest mama bear instincts. Many years ago when Joey was around four, and still fairly early into our adventures in autism, a lot of buzz was going around about this new "chelation cream" that was supposed to help our children excrete toxic chemicals, including mercury, out of their little bodies.

Now, up until that point, the only chelation techniques that I was aware of had involved using invasive IV's or other heavy duty pharmaceuticals. I had not been willing to try those, but this seemed different. This made sense to me…and I wanted to start the treatments YESTERDAY!!

As per usual, we had limited funds available, and insurance would not pay for us to see a "biomedical" practitioner Biomedical doctors (or DAN doctors) are part of the underground world of autism treatment. We were also in the middle of selling our townhouse, so stress levels and money issues were in an even extra frenzied state. I had to be proactive when calling around to see who might prescribe this cream, because I knew we could only afford one office visit, in order to be able to pay for the medication. (The office visit itself would likely cost at least several hundred dollars). I asked direct questions. I specifically said that we wanted to come in for one visit, and leave with a prescription for that cream (which at the time was only available from ONE particular compounding pharmacy, and only delivered through the mail).

Most doctors had a huge waiting list, (which I put us on just in case) and would not commit to prescribing the cream on the first visit anyway. In my mama bear mode though, nothing is impossible. I kept calling around until I found a doctor that said that he would accommodate my request. Great!! In retrospect, the fact that he didn't have a waiting list, and answered the phone himself, probably should have served as some clue to his legitimacy, but I WANTED TO GET MY HANDS ON THAT CREAM!! I honestly thought that this little bottle was going to cure my son, so of course I was willing to take a leap of faith with the doctor...He was just a required hurdle between me and that cream.

So little Joey and I headed to downtown Chicago for our appointment the following week. We got there, we sat down, and this ass face started to tell me that he was going to have to run many expensive tests on Joey before he could possibly prescribe the cream, and he would need us to come back a couple more times!! Are you freakin' kidding me!!!!! We had already paid about $400 dollars for this visit, (when we "checked in") and I was not any closer to getting what I wanted!! I was LIVID!! I gave that "doctor" a little piece of my mind, and left his office in a fury. Poor Joey. Poor me. Unbelievable!!

As fate would have it though, a couple days later, one of the offices that I had called the previous week had called us with a cancellation. The spot was ours if we wanted it. We wanted it. How would I pay for it?? Hmm. Didn't matter. I would have booked a trip to the moon at that point if I thought it would get us that cream.

SOOO...to make a really long story slightly shorter, we went to the other doctor, they prescribed the cream (along with about a million dollars' worth of vitamins and mineral supplements that he would have to take along with it) and we were on our way. YIPPEEE!!

Interestingly, the next day, I got a phone call from the pharmacy that was filling our prescription. They had gotten a phone call from Dr. Ass Face, telling them not to honor any prescription called in on mine or Joey's behalf, because he suspected that I had STOLEN his freakin' prescription pad!!!!!!! Of course I had NOT done such a thing!!!

We got everything straightened out with the new doctor, and started the treatments, but JEEEEZZZ!!!! I guess I convinced him that I would get that cream come hell or high water…What a tool. Grrrrr. Oh and by the way, it's a sucky reality, but if the cream had worked, I would probably be writing a completely different book right now. Big sigh again.

34. "Ok, Ma'am…Your appointment will be in a year and a half."…

A year and a half in the life of any child is a long time, but when you think there is someone that can really help you treat your child's autism, and you have to wait that long, it's an excruciating eternity.

Everything in the autism world is word of mouth. Mostly from parents, and rarely, if ever, from any source that might be considered "mainstream". It's like its own subculture. Quite bizarre considering the numbers, but true nonetheless. So when one particular doctor's name kept coming up time and time again, I took notice and got on the list.

Time passed, as it does, and the appointment date was getting closer. I received a phone call stating that they would need their check for $1000 to hold our appointment. I knew it was coming, but I did not have the money. Oy. Crazy stress. But in any case, I was NOT giving up our spot.

I literally dropped the check in a public mailbox without knowing how in the world I was going to cover it. I kissed the envelope, wished it luck, and waved goodbye. I had faith that somehow, it would all work out...and it did. The check was covered by a kind soul, and we had our appointment.

We were scheduled for 8:00am on a weekday, about 2 hours south of our house. We were going to have to get a hotel room down there to be on time. So off we went, me and my Joey, excited for our newest adventure. We had never stayed alone in a hotel together, and that part was really fun. We went out for a bite to eat, watched TV, and had a good time. The hotel was only about half a mile from the doctor's office, so I had peace of mind, knowing we would be on time.

Morning came quickly, and we went out to the car, and guess what?? We had a FLAT TIRE!! Pfffft. Seriously?? Anyway, I marched us into that car as if nothing was wrong, and drove that half mile down to the doctor's office. The tire could wait, we however, had waited long enough.

I wish I had a really happy ending to this story, one that said that this doctor was all that we had hoped for, but sadly, that was not the case. We continued on the gf/cf diet, tried a lot of different supplements, tests and what not over the next year or so with her, not seeing much improvement. Eventually, the financial component made it impossible for us to continue with her services, and we had to move on.

***PLEASE NOTE: THE FOLLOWING 6 STORIES ARE RELATED, AND ARE IN CHRONOLOGICAL ORDER.

35. Please don't hold the Mayo...Our visit to The Mayo Clinic (#1 of 6)

We had gotten our sweet boy on Mayo Clinic's waiting list about 6 months prior to our visit. During that waiting time, Joey started on that expensive cream and supplement therapy, we had found the house we wanted to buy,(our house with the awesome yard), put our townhouse up for sale, found mold in the attic of said townhouse when new buyer had an inspection, got stuck paying a crap load of money to have it professionally cleaned, got less $$$ than we wanted for the sale, were charged an unexpected extra couple thousand dollars by our mortgage broker at the closing on our new house, and then, just for fun, doubled our mortgage and all of our utility bills with no cushion left to help us adjust. Yep!! We sure did.

We were a little nervous to double our bills, but it felt just like 5 years earlier when we first bought the townhouse. We knew we'd be kind of broke, but it seemed worth it to get our dream house for our family. We had no idea what was about to hit us financially, but I'll get into more detail on that a little later.

So anyway, 2 months after moving into our new house, it was time for our trip to The Mayo Clinic in Rochester, MN. It's about 5 hours away by car, they take most insurance, and it's where generations of my family have gone whenever there have been unusual or scary health concerns.

By this point, Joey had just turned 5, he was enrolled in an "autism preschool program" through our county's special education district, and we were pretty darn sure that he had autism. Basically, we went to Mayo to get the "official" diagnosis, and to make sure that a duck, was indeed a duck .SOOOO…we dropped our almost two year old baby Shayna at my parent's house, and off Darin, Joey and I went on our adventure.

Mayo Clinic is set up in such a way that everything happens rather quickly. Instead of waiting weeks in between appointments with assorted professionals, you are given a schedule that crams everything into a much shorter period of time. We were scheduled for three, VERY FULL days of testing, poking, prodding, fasting, blood taking, etc., etc., etc…NOT exactly fun for anybody, but particularly not for one five year old with autism, and his ferociously protective mama bear. It was really hard on all of us, but a necessary evil.

On the final day, we were scheduled for what Mayo refers to as a, "Core Conference". This is when all of the M.D.s, therapists, psychologists, psychiatrists, neurologists, etc. etc. etc. met with us to discuss their conclusions and to make recommendations. By this point, they had also spoken to several representatives from Joey's preschool to get an idea of how he was functioning in that setting as well.

I wasn't really expecting to hear anything surprising at that meeting. Basically, I expected them to fully confirm the autism diagnosis, and I thought that would be that…I was wrong. Yes, they did confirm the diagnosis, although they said the word "severe" which I had not anticipated, but then, after a lot of technical talk, which to be honest, was hard for this non-scientific headed mama to process, there was one sentence that would forever change the trajectory of our lives. The lead physician looked at me and said, "Joey's current school placement is where you would want him to be if you had no hope of him improving."

Um…WHAT??!!!!!! WHAT????!!!!!!! But he was in an "autism program". Shouldn't they know what they're doing??!!! There are no words that could possibly describe how I felt at that moment. Completely hollow and hopeless. I had no idea what to think or feel. I had a fire lit under me. I felt like a jolt of electricity had just gone through my entire body. When I look back on that moment, I am so unbelievably grateful to that horribly blunt doctor. They went on to give us some paperwork on the types of therapies and programs that have had proven results for kids with autism. They told us that Joey MUST have these types of services in order to improve. MUST?? Well then, he will get them!!!!

We got home from Mayo, called an emergency I.E.P. Meeting, and asked that Joey be given these services that Mayo recommended. They shuffled some papers, causally looked up at me, and said that it looked like he was doing just fine in his current placement, and that they were not going to accommodate my request at that time. Um…WHAT?? Didn't you hear me?? He NEEDS these things. They blew me off like I knew nothing (Which at the time, I only knew next to nothing, but what I did know was that my son WOULD be getting what he needed, and SOON!!) SOOO… I stood up, and informed them that we would be hiring an attorney and scheduling a follow up emergency meeting. And so it begins…

36. The fight, the attorney, the private therapy, and the debt debt debt...(#2 of 6)

As I said earlier, we were already in kind of a scary financial state, even before beginning our next adventure, but I saw no choice. We had to fight that school district, and we had to mean business. I was quite certain that they would not provide Joey with any of the necessary services unless we made them. We couldn't really afford any help, but I was not going to let that stand in the way of my boy's future. I had to do everything that I possibly could to get him on the right track.

So what's a mama bear to do? Well, first, we found an attorney. He required a hefty retainer that I took out as a cash advance on a credit card. Ok. Done. What next? Hmmm. My Joey needed those services, and I had to start somewhere, so...I found a private therapy center. My intention was to eventually have our school district pay for his therapy, but until then, somehow we were going to have to pay for it ourselves.

Unfortunately, it was about $150 an hour to see the behavior analysts, and about $50 an hour with the therapists. Both were required. Mayo said that Joey should have 40 hours of therapy per week, but once again, insurance didn't cover jack. Ugh. We would get as many hours as possible. I maxed out several credit cards over the next few months, thinking of course, that I would soon be reimbursed by the school district. $$$$$$$$$$. Things were beginning to happen.

The next IEP meeting was to be very important, to say the least. I prepared for that meeting as if I was going to the Supreme Court. Our attorney had advised us to schedule it a bit further down the road, to allow us time to prepare. So prepare we did!! Data, data, data. That is what I compiled and focused on for the next couple months.

I was picking Joey up half way through the school day, every day (with my little Shayna Bug in tow), and then driving about 45 minutes to his 3 hour therapy sessions. He had an amazing therapist who was wonderful with him, and he was making some progress. It was going well!!

We had quite the dream team going for our upcoming meeting. On the list for our side was our attorney, Joey's fabulous new therapist with all of her data showing how well he was doing, Mayo Clinic would be on the phone, and then of course, ME!! (and of course Darin was there too).

I had ripped his current school's data apart piece by piece, and it was very clear that he was NOT doing "just fine". In fact, he was not getting what he needed at all!! Our case was very clear, and there was really no room for any of their bureaucratic gobbly gook arguments. You could hear a pin drop in that meeting when we were finished. They had NOTHING to say. It was fantastic. They asked to meet again in a few weeks. That was their only response.

Over the next several months, their lawyer became increasingly useless, and was doing nothing but standing in the way of any real progress. We would meet, he would yell some absurd things, and then we would schedule another meeting. He was extremely unprofessional. One day, he actually told our lawyer to "Go f#!k himself"…that was the straw that broke this mama's back. I was livid!! This guy was standing directly in the path between my son and his progress. I would have no more of it!!

The next day, on our way home from dropping Joey off at school, both of us in pajamas and pony tails, my two year old Shayna and I found ourselves driving past the school superintendent's office. He was the one that would make the final decision on what they would, and would not provide for Joey. All of the people at the IEP meetings were there working for him. He and I however, had never met.

I pulled into the parking lot, Shayna and I walked up to the receptionist's desk, and asked her to please tell the superintendent that we would like to meet with him. It was time to let him meet the "Crazy Mrs. Mitchell" that I was sure he had heard so much about. After all, that horrible lawyer was representing HIS school district! He should know what was going on.

So we were lead into his office, PJ's, ponytails and all, and he asked us to sit down. I introduced myself and my daughter (who had now started playing with items on his desk), and began to tell him our story, which of course ended up with a little bit of the ugly cry, and telling him that his lawyer had told my lawyer to "Go f#%k himself". So here's this big head honcho guy, at work one morning, and suddenly he's in an impromptu meeting with a crying mom in pajamas, and a two year old playing with the stuff on his desk. Life is strange.

Anyway, by the end of the week, they had fired that horrible lawyer, hired a new one, and called us back for "mediation". That meeting ended without any resolution, but their new lawyer called me back for a private meeting the next day. It was cut and dry. He had told his clients that if we went to court, they would surely lose. He presented me with their offer right then and there. It stated that they would pay for Joey to attend a "private therapeutic day school" that we had chosen, in which he could get the services that were needed...but they would not pay for any services that had already been rendered before starting at the new school in the Fall.

Doing the math, one year of private school would have cost more than we were out for the private therapy, and that was only for one year. We took the deal, and they have been paying for his "private placement" for the last seven years.

(He has changed private schools a few times, but I'll get into that a little later).

As much of financial mess that all of these events created, I would do it all again in a heartbeat. Thankfully, the important players in our school district seem to know that as well.

37. We won!! Now what? The little car that couldn't, but somehow did it anyway.(#3 of 6)

Special education law requires that school districts provide transportation to and from school for every student…private placements out of their home district included.

When our battle ended, it was already summertime, and we were poised and ready for Joey to start his new school in the Fall. He would need to travel an hour away from our house each and every day, but distance was not nearly as important to me as programming (and continues to be more important as you will see a little later).

Now, keep in mind, at that time, Joey was only starting Kindergarten. He was five years old, and not very verbal. He was such a little munchkin, and even though the district was required to pay for his transportation, I was just not mentally or physically capable of sending him off on his own for an hour long ride with some stranger.

So what's a mama bear to do? Well, I took my crappy car, with my Joey, my two year old, and myself…loaded up, and drove him to school each and every day for an entire school year. We left our house at 8:00am, and got him to school at 9:00. Shayna and I would be home by 10:00, and then leave our house again by 2:00, and pick him up at 3:00. Every single day...and don't even get me started on field trip days!! Ugh.

Our district did reimburse me a certain dollar amount per mile for gas, but they only paid for one round trip, and we were taking two.

Anyway, to make our situation just a little bit extra fun and exciting, when I say I had a "crappy" car, that is quite possibly the biggest understatement EVER. We were SOOOOO broke at that time, that anything that ever broke on that car, had to stay broken, such as: 1) The horn didn't work. 2) The front, right turn signal did not work. 3) There was no washer fluid reservoir, so I had to throw water onto the windshield from a bottle (which would freeze in the winter). 4) I had a very hard time getting up any kind of hill because the car would just decide it was not strong enough to make it. (Thankfully we didn't live in the mountains). 5) The car would often die when sitting still (stoplights, trains, etc.) 6) My husband broke the switch for the windshield wipers, and I had to poke a piece of plastic in there a certain way to get the wipers to turn on (which was fantastic when it was already raining and I couldn't see). 7) The back driver's side seatbelt had unexpectedly decided to eat Joey one day, requiring me to use scissors to get him out of its ever tightening grasp. From that day forward, he had to sit too close to Shayna. There's probably more, but I may have blocked it out of my mind.

It was horrible and dangerous to drive that thing, but truth be told, we worked so hard to get him into that private school, I would have driven that kid to the moon on a bicycle if I had to, and I would do it all again in a heartbeat.

38. Another new school, a little leap of faith, and the best driver ever!! (#4 of 6)

As high as my hopes had been for Joey's new school, it didn't work out as I had imagined, and the following summer I found myself searching for a different program. I had thought that the hardest part was over when our school district agreed to pay for private placement, but as it turned out, there's often more than one hardest part in the world of autism.

The new school was still an hour away, only in a different direction. I did not see how I could possibly continue to drive him every day. Shayna was unhappy, I was stressed to the max, and Joey was getting a little bit older. SOOO...enter the transportation company.

Our school district would hire a transportation company to take Joey to and from school. I was a COMPLETE nervous wreck. If only he would be able to tell me how he was being treated!! It was such a long ride, and I was terrified for him. But I saw no other option.

So the big day arrived... The red minivan pulled up on our driveway, ready to take my baby to his new school. I was ready to throw up. I had spoken to the driver on the phone a couple of times prior to that day, just to give her a little bit of background on Joey's issues. I wanted her to be aware of some of his likes/dislikes/triggers etc. before she was on the road with him. She seemed nice.

So I walked him out to the van, officially introduced myself to the driver, buckled him in, and with tears in my eyes, waved goodbye to my precious boy...and then threw Shayna in the car and followed them all the way to school on that first day!! Haha!! (Are you shocked?? I didn't think so).

The driver ended up being the sweetest lady in the world, and she loved my Joey very much. She would show him cows and horses on the road, play his favorite music, and even schedule her vacation time around his school calendar. She was always on time, never took a sick day, and was his wonderful driver for the next four years. The school however, would still change a couple more times.

39. Another school, a lying selfish woman, and a giant step toward our future... (#5 of 6)

Joey's second private placement had gone fairly well, but after two years, he was aging out of their program. By this point, we were near the end of his second grade year. So the search was on once again.

A few months earlier, a new private school for autism had opened only 30 minutes from our house. I was interested to see what they might have to offer, so I made an appointment. I was excited by the idea that he might be able to attend school closer to home.

It was opened by two moms, both with kids on the spectrum. They talked a good game. They had gone through many hoops and hurdles with their own kids, and in the end, decided to help others as well by opening their own school. It felt right. Looking back, I was probably too quick to trust them, but they were moms like me...they understood the frustration and anguish, right? Ummm...Nope. Apparently not.

Observations were scheduled, meetings planned, and Joey was all set to attend the Summer session at his current school, and then begin his new school in the Fall.

By this point, he had already developed some aggressive behaviors that required special attention by extra staff, and many of those behaviors would historically "spike" during the summer.

The owner of the new school, this "woman", and fellow mother of a child with autism, looked me straight in the eye and said, "I really think he should start with us during the Summer. We'd rather start to work with him at his worst rather than at his best."

I was impressed with her thinking. I thought that she may have a good idea. It would give Joey a fresh start, and possibly some new skills to deal with his increasing summer frustrations. I agreed to start him there for summer school.

My sweet, wonderful and complicated boy was only in attendance at that SHAM of a school for 3 days , when the owners called me in for a meeting. They went on to strongly recommend that Joey be seen by a psychiatrist, and be started on anti-psychotic medications. Ummm...WHAT?? You just met my kid, you had me pull him out of a successful program, and now you want me to drug him so you can handle him??

I was shocked and horrified, sad and uncertain. I was not at all sure what to do. Up until that point, I had never tried any drugs to help with Joey's aggression. It's not that I had never considered the idea that he may benefit from them, but I had never decided take that next step.

Once again, they talked a good game, and I came around to thinking that maybe I should at least investigate the idea. Two days later, they told me that Joey would not be allowed to come back to school until he was on some sort of medication. Pffffft. Seriously???

Hearing myself tell this story now, I can't believe that my next step was indeed to take my sweet boy to a psychiatrist to get him on medication. Ugh. But that's what I did.

By this point, he had been home from school for about two weeks. I was under the impression that Joey could return after they received the report from the psychiatrist, stating our plan of action for the medications… but apparently, I misunderstood that lying, selfish, bitch. Ugh. What she meant to say, was that she was going to string me along for the next 3 months, never let Joey back into her school, but continue to collect tuition checks from our school district until she "officially" kicked him out.

Wow. Oh...and the psychiatrist that we went to also sucked (recommended of course by the same lovely lady), and we discontinued all medications because Joey was worse on the meds than he had been before. Good times.

As with many things in life though, in those dark moments, I could not yet see the good that would soon come from this experience. The footsteps on the path to our next adventure were now set in motion.

40. Maybe some things really do happen for a reason? (#6 of 6)

After three months of "waiting" for Joey to go back to school, I was suddenly faced with the reality that I had to find him yet ANOTHER new program. I had to start from scratch, and it was already the Fall of what should have been his third grade year.

I went to EVERY school that I thought might have a program for my boy. I would research a program, make an appointment, go and take a "tour", go out to my car and cry, go home, and repeat the process. You would not believe some of the places that I toured; the types of people trying to "schmooze" me into signing Joey up for their completely inappropriate programs. It was horrible!! I was starting to lose it a little.

Was there REALLY nowhere for him to go? Would I be forced to "home school" him? Home school was not the answer…my kid needed to learn how to understand other people too, not just me. He needed the social components. I was at my wits end.

Up until this point, I had only looked at programs that were within a one hour radius of our house. However, the day soon came when I realized that I had exhausted ALL possibilities within those search parameters. By this point, I believe we were already into October, and Joey had been out of school since June.

One hopeless and frustrating Saturday night, I struggled with myself, but eventually came to the realization that I was going to have to open up my search area to include schools that were further away. It finally clicked. I had a new search plan started. and would continue first thing in the morning.

Sunday morning came quickly on no sleep. I resumed my research on the computer, looking at schools that were a little bit further away. My list of places to contact was growing, and then I received a text from my aunt. A text that that one day earlier may have gone unnoticed, or may have seemed unimportant. The text simply said, "There's an autism school on the front page of the Sunday paper, thought you might find it interesting", or something to that effect.

I swear only a few moments later, there was a little story about a school for autism on the local morning news. I looked at my list, and what do you know? The school on the news was on my list from the night before.

I ran out and bought the Sunday paper, read the article, and was absolutely FLOORED...Once again, the same school! This place sounded PERFECT for my Joey!! Talk about crazy timing and divine intervention!!

All of this happened less than 12 hours after my decision to look into schools a little further away.

I called them first thing Monday morning, and was down there, an hour and fifteen minutes from our house, in person by that same afternoon. As it turned out, this school had been at a different location for nearly 10 years, but had just purchased a HUGE brand new, state of the art building to accommodate their growing population.

They had not even been accepting new applicants for quite some time, they simply did not have the space...until that moment!! I think Joey may have been one of their first potential new students.

Anyway, if I had discovered them ANY earlier, I would have thought they were too far away, and they would have told me that they were not accepting new students. But instead, the way the universe works, by the time I pulled up to that amazing building, wide eyed and excited on that Monday afternoon, I had goose bumps and tears in my eyes, and knew in my heart that my search was over.

They invited me to their ribbon cutting ceremony that was to take place on that upcoming Wednesday, and the rest as they say, is history.

His ride is one hour and fifteen minutes each way with no traffic...and worth every single second. I no longer worry about him during his school day. In fact, sometimes, I even forget that he is off on a field trip somewhere, and that says A LOT!! We sure have come a long way, Baby!!

They are an amazing group of people with an amazing program. Joey is doing very well there, and has been in attendance for the past 4 years. Their program runs all the way through high school, and they have even implemented an adult program.

I cannot say enough about how grateful I am to all of the wonderful staff and administration at his school. Joey and I have made some bonds so strong, that they will likely last a lifetime. We are truly blessed to have found them, and I thank god for them daily.

41. The 200 year old rug on our wall…Yeah, I know.

About six years ago, my now 99 year old grandfather gave me a rug/tapestry of sorts, and told me that it had belonged to my grandmother. She had gotten it from her mother, and it was likely brought over on "the boat" from Russia.

He said he didn't have any use for it, and it had just been sitting, collecting dust in a closet for the last 50 years or so. Well, it matched my living room perfectly, so I decided to take it, and hang it on my living room wall, behind one of our couches. It was perfect for that spot! I loved it!!

Anyway, the years had taken their toll on the "tassels" that were hanging around the edges, and they were falling off quite easily. One day, when I walked into the living room, to my surprise, ALL of the tassels were off, and Joey had a mess of 200 + year old thread hanging out of his mouth. Oy!

Ok, well now that the tassels were off, I figured we could keep it up without any further obsession from my boy. I kept it up on the wall, and enjoyed it very much for just about the next six years…UNTIL…one day about 6 months ago.

For some reason, he became obsessed with it again, and

kept knocking it down. He would pull at the side and make it sway. Since the fabric is so old and fragile, every time he did this, it would fall down. So now, it is back in a closet, collecting dust, until I can figure out how to "Joey proof" it. I know...Wish me luck.

42. Vacuum Cleaners...

Joey has a love/hate relationship with vacuum cleaners. He hates how loud they are, but he loves the wires and hoses. He watches me vacuum with this funny look on his face, covering his ears even over the headphones, but usually smiling as he watches it go back and forth. He particularly loves it when it is not in use. My Joey has been personally responsible for our need to replace at least two vacuum cleaners. He chewed and pulled out the wires so badly, that I used to have to step around the frayed parts while vacuuming for fear of electrocuting myself (we couldn't afford a new one at the time, and hey...it still worked). Knock on wood, he hasn't zoned in our newest one just yet. Yay!

43. Tornado warnings and autism are a great combination...said nobody ever!

I don't know about you, but to my knowledge, until recently, a "tornado warning" meant that a tornado had been spotted nearby, and you should seek shelter immediately. On the other hand, a "tornado watch" was issued when conditions were such that a tornado could possibly develop.

Apparently, the criteria for both have changed, and I can pretty much 100% guarantee you that whoever is responsible for this change, DOES NOT have a child with severe autism!! UGH.

I think it all started the Spring before last. It seemed like a typical stormy, rainy, April , and I'm not exactly SURE what happened, but I'm guessing that somebody at the National Weather Service got a new toy.

We had tornado warning after tornado warning, and even during the announcement that was telling us to go to the basement, it would say, "this storm is 'capable' of producing tornadoes". Do you have any idea what my son with severe autism, who is prone to aggressive meltdowns is "CAPABLE" of when we wake him up from a dead sleep to drag him down into the basement for no reason??? Somebody better have spotted a freakin' tornado or this mama ,who now has a much bigger storm on her hands, is gonna be pissed!!

 I now watch the radar myself, and we listen a little more closely to what is ACTUALLY going on…But I can't stand the way they have started to "cry wolf" when they shouldn't. The warning system is way too valuable to misuse that way. Oh well…what can ya do? Always an adventure!!

44. The fundraiser and the pooping machine…

As you know, Darin and I don't get out very often, so when the first fundraiser for Joey's amazing new school came around, I was very excited. Not only would we get to have a fancy night out, but it was also for the best cause ever!!

Tickets were a pre-paid, non-refundable, $100 each, but somehow we scraped it together, and were set for our big date. His suit was pressed, I had a pretty dress, my parents were more than willing to come babysit, and it was going to be a great night. Right? Pffft.

Well, it started off perfectly fine. I took a shower, did my hair, and put on some makeup. I was feeling good. Since I usually get hot when I'm getting dressed up, I leave the clothes and accessories for last.

So there I was, hair done, make up on, and had actually just put on a pair of nylons when suddenly....I smelled something awful.

I walked into Joey's room to find that the poor kid had a HORRIBLE case of diarrhea. I opened his windows, sprayed some Lysol, changed him, changed his sheets, and hoped it was just a one-time event.

It happened again. Oy! So I sent Darin off to Walgreens, suit and all, to pick up some tummy medicine.

I was pretty sure that this Cinderella was not going to the ball after-all. I gave him the medicine, my parents arrived, and I was not all sure what to do.

I waited. I gave him the second dose and waited some more. We went about a half hour without any pooping. Yes! I gave him a lot of water and some crackers, and put a durable plastic cover on his mattress. I kissed my boy goodbye, and hoped for the best.

We were late getting to the banquet which was an hour and a half away from our house, but we did get there. That first drink from the open bar went down very easily, I tell ya!!

We stayed for dinner but not much else. I called my parents to check on the kids, and they were both asleep, but I couldn't help feeling like I needed to go home. So we did.

I'm sure that the night has become more memorable as a result of the poopy adventure, but I hear that sometimes an uneventful, completely forgettable evening can be fun too. A girl can dream, right?

45. Puberty?? Oh the joy...

The biggest change in Joey, aside from the obvious physical changes that puberty brings, has been my sweet boy's level of cooperation.
He used to follow any direction I gave him (to the best of his ability). He would always try to do what I was asking.

Now, he thinks about it first, and understands that he actually has a choice in the matter. For example, in the past, whenever I would hold out my hand and ask him to give me whatever inappropriate, inedible or unsafe object he was playing with, he would hand it right over. Now, he stops what he's doing momentarily, stares at me for a second, and sometimes walks the other way, or just continues on with what he's doing as if I had said nothing!! Are you kidding??

I have to say though, at the same time that these new antics drive me nuts, I love it when he displays "typical" thirteen year old boy behavior. It may be under different circumstances than most, but it is still teenage defiance at its best.

46. Time For School!!

There are several possible scenarios for a school day morning around our house. They pretty much range from uneventful, to awful. Most of the time, everything goes smoothly, we all get out of the house on time and go about our day. When things go awry… well that's a different story.

I always take my daughter to the bus first. She hates waking up and getting ready , but I usually manage to get her to the bus on time.

Now, Joey, on the other hand, takes a minivan to school,

and he is the only passenger. Thank goodness he has always had an understanding driver because our assorted morning scenarios can cause us to be quite late getting out onto the driveway.

For example; Scenario #1) He usually wakes up on his own on school days, but on the rare occasion that he doesn't, he may possibly pull the old, "I'm still sleeping, and if you wake me up, I might have a HUGE meltdown and be even later for school" trick.

This scenario is tons of fun because I have to get really creative with my "accidental" noises that are specifically designed to wake him up, without him knowing that I'm doing it on purpose. (Opening and closing doors and cabinets, running the water, turning up my TV, coughing, etc.)

Once I hear that he is awake, I wait until I hear some happy noises before I am sure I can go in to give him his morning medicines. If all goes well, he is usually OK to get up and dressed at that point.

Scenario #2) The "Something is really bothering me, and I am SOOOO frustrated and angry because I woke up like this!!" scenario. When the morning begins with him in this state, he will likely bang on his walls and come into my room very angry.

Now this does not make for a good start to anyone's day. Poor guy. I usually attribute this behavior to some kind of physical pain he is experiencing, but cannot express. (I'll talk about these episodes a little bit more in depth later).

It hurts me both mentally and physically to see him so upset, while at the same time, I am required to quickly transition from sound asleep to superhero, all in the blink of an eye. With this scenario, a little break so he can get himself together usually helps. He needs some space to calm down.

Sometimes he needs a little Pepto or Tylenol, depending on what my best guess is as to what's bothering him. I try to keep his driver posted on our progress towards getting dressed and out the door, but sometimes we are REALLY late.

Scenario #3) The "Surprise!! I'm really really dirty and I need a very long impromptu bath before going to school this morning" trick. No need for more details on this one, but let's just say that this scenario can be quite time consuming.

Anyway, there are many more possible situations that could arise during our morning routine, but I think you get the idea.

47. Team Joey

Over the years, my Joey has wiggled and bounced his way into countless hearts. This child is truly adored by many. Who can resist those gorgeous big blue eyes?

I think he brings out the best in the people that are there to help him. He is not an easy case, and has moments that many could not, or simply would not, choose to handle. It takes a special kind of person to see all that is so wonderful about my precious boy…but once they see it, they never, ever forget it.

From current and former teachers, assistants, and support staff, to therapists, school nurses, and bus drivers. From pharmacists, technicians and even one or two doctors, to of course all of our own family, friends, and loved ones…there is a lot of love and support out there for this amazing kid, and for that, this mama will be forever grateful.

48. He's Late!!!

When I chose his school, I made a deal with myself. I decided that when I thought that the weather was not ok for travel (snowstorms, ice, heavy fog, etc.) that I would keep him home, whether or not the school actually closed. I will also have him picked up early when I see that weather will be developing once he is already there.

Most of the time, this allows me to avoid my tendency to over think his travels. As much progress as I have made over the years, however, I still worry about my boy. It's a very long ride, and he still cannot communicate. So to put it simply, when he is late, I freak the hell out.

I know, I'm not proud of it, but I can't seem to help myself. Every awful scenario starts running through my head, and by the time he gets home, I am exhausted, and need a glass of wine. Thankfully it doesn't happen that often. This is the price I pay for his awesome school, I guess.

49. Contest for best "Heinz Ketchup" commercial...

I am always making up silly lyrics for songs, whether it's for Joey, or just because my mind is wired that way, it happens all the time. So when I saw an ad for a contest to make a Heinz Ketchup commercial, I actually already had the perfect song that I had made up a year earlier!! How funny is that??!!

It's a parody of Barry Manilow's "Copa Cabana". We made a video of my kids eating ketchup, and you hear me singing this song in the background. My entry was actually disqualified because I used a parody, but here it is for your amusement...bet it gets stuck in your head too!!

"His name is Joey...He loves Heinz Ketchup. He'd do any-thing for Heinz Ketchup. He'll get some ketchup on his chair, and even ketchup in his hair. His name is Joey...He loves Heinz Ketch-up. French fries his passion, on burgers it's smashin'…It's Heinz Ketch-up. Eat it up yuuumm".

50. The drive-thru doctor...

When either of my kids get sick, it kills me…but when Joey gets sick, it is even more heartbreaking. The poor guy can't even tell me what's wrong, and I always have to guess. I am the best guesser in the universe, but it is still just a guess.

I am not a "run to the doctor" kind of mom. I am much more of a wait and see kind of girl… but when you gotta go, you gotta go.

Under the BEST circumstances, even when he isn't horribly sick, Joey does NOT like going to the doctor (me either!) When he doesn't feel well though, it can be a heck of a lot worse. One time a year or two ago, the poor kid was so sick, and seemed to me to be having pain in his ears. I knew I had to take him, so off we went.

We made it out of the car and into the office ok, but then they took us in to the blood pressure and weighing area (which I no longer allow them to do first). He proceeded to COMPLETELY freak out. A huge meltdown in the middle of the doctor's office. He was pulling my hair, pinching, kicking, etc. All of this before the doctor had even had a chance to examine him.

I had no choice but to take my sick boy back out to my car. I buckled him in, and waited for him to calm down. Then, I had quite an unconventional idea. I knew he most likely needed an antibiotic (even though I hate them), and I did not want to take him home without a prescription. There was absolutely no way that I was bringing him back inside to get all worked up again.

So what's a mama bear to do? Well, I called the doctor's

office from my car, and asked the doctor if she would please, please, please come outside and quickly examine my poor guy in the back seat of my minivan. She said YES!!

She came out, did a quick once over, and prescribed an antibiotic for his infected ears and throat. Once again, a random act of kindness in the middle of a horrible and hopeless situation brought happy tears to this mama's eyes.

You just never know how some people will surprise you and rise to the occasion, and I was more than grateful.

51. Your son keeps eating the Play-Doh...

This was a recurring theme in Joey's preschool years. From his very first class until he was about five, every time I would pick him up, the teacher would tell me that he had eaten some play-doh.

Guess what? He's thirteen now, and I'm pretty sure he would still taste it if it were placed in front of him. It's just one of those crazy things that MOST kids grow out of I guess. Maybe it's hereditary? For some reason, I know what Play-doh tastes like...Do you?

52. The waiting room...

Oh yes, the "waiting room". A room with no other purpose than to wait. Doesn't that sound like a great place for my Joey? Not so much. It's not that he isn't capable of waiting patiently, it's just that waiting rooms are generally crowded, busy, and noisy, with a lot of different people doing a lot of different things.

These places are primarily used for the dreaded 'transition" of each and every person visiting that particular office. Transitions are sometimes difficult for Joey, and if he is already slightly agitated, this is the time when a meltdown will likely occur. So you can imagine his stress level when you add crying children, ringing phones, coughing and sneezing adults, and other assorted noises to the mix.

For example, our last trip to the neurologist's office. We have to travel downtown, which takes over an hour. We valet the car, but still have to make our way through a busy office building, walk by a pastry cart, (which he gets to have a treat from on the way out), wait for the elevator, get on the elevator with other people, go up seven floors with all of the wonderful dinging and starting and stopping that an elevator in a busy downtown office building tends to do, get out and walk to the office, and THEN we are finally in the glorious "waiting room". Oy. If that's not a setup…sheesh.

Anyway, on this particular day, we walked in and it was much more crowded than normal. We sat down, I pulled out my "bag of tricks" that I always pack for these types of activities, and hoped for the best. I had his favorite string toy, tons of snacks, water, music, etc.

We were actually doing quite well considering the crowd, but the wait time became unusually long. Then, it happened. A little two year old boy started to throw a fit. I saw it start, and tried to be proactive by moving us across the room.

Joey seemed to be dealing with it fairly well, he was irritated, but still in control. UNTIL… a second child began to cry. That was it!! He freaked!! Stomping, pinching, hitting, scratching me, etc. So fun.

Thankfully, as I always try to do, I had a plan in my head just in case this were to occur. They have single stall bathrooms in this office, so we made our way back to one of them. I was able to safely sit him in there for the few minutes it took him to calm down. It was quiet, and comforting for him to be away from the craziness and noise.

I however, was now a shaking nervous wreck. A nurse came up to ask if we were ok, but she could tell that I was a bit shaken. She hung out for a minute, and then told me that our office was ready.

Ok...Great! Much more comfy than the bathroom. "Come on honey, let's go". Another lesson learned. Apparently this office needs to be added to the list of "call ahead" places, to make sure we have a successful visit. Yep. Next time we will be going straight into our own space. Hmm.

53. One kid's pleasure is another kid's pain...

I always try to walk the line between over doing it with Joey, (which can often result in some "challenging" behaviors), and depriving him of new and different experiences. He does not like things that are hectic, crowded and noisy, which would exclude almost all "kid friendly" outings if avoiding those things was the only criteria.

This line of course is also compounded and blurred by my desire to do fun things as a family, while also trying not to deprive Shayna of the fun things that she wants to do. Add to this scenario, weekend activities with one husband that can sometimes be a tad opinionated himself, and there you have it.

I don't want anyone to miss out on anything. It's not easy, but I usually believe that where there's a will, there's a way. So over the years, I have done my best to become as resourceful and creative as possible when planning our activities.

As with many things in our crazy life, and as you will see in the next few stories, sometimes my plans work out great, and sometimes, to put it mildly...they don't.

54. Apple Picking...

I absolutely LOVED going apple picking as a kid, and I get totally warm and fuzzy sharing that experience with my own kids. But somehow, over recent years, the apple picking experience has morphed into some sort of chaotic, line waiting, face painting, hay riding, bounce housing, donut eating, child screaming, money grabbing commercial activity. It became something that was really stressful.

Now if Joey did not have the issues that he does, I may have been forced to accept this new entity, but he could not handle the craziness. So this mama, not willing to give up her tradition of yearly apple picking with her babies, had to find a solution.

Through necessity, and word of mouth due to my complaining, we found the BEST APPLE ORCHARD EVER!!! Do you want to know why it's the best? Because the only thing there, is an APPLE ORCHARD!! Rows and rows of nothing but apple trees. It is so wonderful and peaceful, and there is not a bouncy house or hay ride in sight. In fact, they don't even have any buildings!!

We go every year, and both kids love to eat their way through the whole thing. It's tons of fun, all you pay for is the apples. We now have our own little family tradition of apple picking, and let me tell you...perfection.

55. Going to the pumpkin farm...

A couple weeks later, it's time for the pumpkin farm!! I love this fall tradition too. Once again, we have tried many different techniques and venues over the years, some with success, some not so much.

I'm open to the bouncy houses, face painting, donuts, etc. for this adventure, but I don't want to spend a million dollars on admission, just to have to leave at a moment's notice if Joey has a meltdown. More than once, my husband or myself have had to get off of the hayride in the middle of a pumpkin field, and walk back to the farm with Joey fighting us in a massive meltdown the whole way. Not fun. I think it was just too much for him to process.

When you have paid $50 or more in admission for a day of "fun" with your family, and you have to leave suddenly and prematurely, it makes it kind of hard to get excited about trying again the next time.

A few years ago we found a family run farm that is smaller than the other money pits, where face painting, hayride, bouncy house, corn maze, petting zoo, etc. are all unlimited, and all included for just $4 a kid!! Amazing what you can find when you look!!

They have had our business ever since. Such a great deal, and then of course we spend our money in their store, buying some fresh cider, veggies, corn, apple donuts, etc. We always try to go in the morning so we beat the bulk of the people, and it is usually a great time.

Once again, in another great example of genuine kindness

and understanding, the wonderful people that run that farm even let Joey have some alone time in their bouncy house. So sweet, and he LOVES that thing!! We always come home tired from playing, and quite full of goodies. Now that is a fun family day in my book.

56. Adventures at the mall...

I am not surprised at all by the fact that Shayna loves the mall, she is all girl. She loves the window shopping, having lunch, and all of the typical activities that you might find at any suburban mall. The funny thing is, that Joey has ALWAYS loved the mall too. Before losing much of his speech, when we would drive past, he would look out his car window and say ,"I want mall! I want mall!".

It works for me, I always liked it too. We never spend a ton of money, we really only go to have some fun walking around on a rainy day.

Now sometimes, when I bring both of them, I have a little bit of a problem because they have a completely different "mall technique". Shayna likes to walk a million miles, and never slow down. Joey likes to walk slowly, look around, and stop to sit and rest every so often.

Well one day, Shayna had been nagging me to go into the "Hello Kitty" store to look around. I told her that we could just go in for a minute, and then we'd have to go take a break for Joey. SOOO in we went.

It was a very pink and foofy girl store, and we had dragged our tired boy in there with us. I turned my head for maybe 2 seconds, and when I looked back, Joey had sat down with his butt INSIDE the store's window display, knocking over a few things (luckily they were soft things).

Well, within seconds, there was a panicked group of Asian women working in that store that ran up and started speaking to me in some panicked Asian language that I did not understand. It was such a ridiculous situation that I can't even explain it now without a little chuckle.

Anyway, I quickly put the stuff back up, apologized to the best of my ability, and we made our exit.

My boy. My sweet and innocent little lamb. I'm sorry, honey. That wasn't a bench.

57. Meltdown at Walmart...Just me and my boy

Shopping can go either way with my sweet boy. Sometimes he's fantastic, and sometimes... he's not. Many times I've gotten a little bit of both.

For example, I think it was about a year ago, when I took Joey with me to pick up a list of odds and ends at Walmart. Things were going just fine as we walked up and down the aisles, trying on jackets, buying socks and underwear, etc. We were having a great time.

When we had everything we needed, and a nice full cart, I went to grab a gallon of milk from far back corner of the store. Just as I put the milk in the cart, Joey put his shirt in his mouth and started to get really upset. This was one of the "x factor" upsets, and I had no idea what had upset him.

Nope, this couldn't happen in the front of the store, it had to happen a mile away from the front door, and of course on a day that we were by ourselves. I don't remember the exact circumstances, but I do remember that our cart was full of things that we absolutely needed, and after all that shopping, I was not going to leave that store without our stuff.

SOOO, being the crazy mama that I am, I brought my hitting, scratching, pinching child with me all the way through the store, to the check out, and somehow got a very sweet, but quite freaked out cashier to ring us up REALLY fast… all while I was fighting off my poor upset boy, who was doing some serious damage to my arms.

I managed to pay, thank the cashier, and get us out to the car with all of our stuff. These are the types of events that earn me my mama stripes. Crazy!!

58. Ho Ho Holy miserable mall rats, Batman…

The mall at Christmas time tends to be a tad nuts, but we enjoy the lights and the music, etc., so I usually take the kids for a little holiday fun during their winter break.

Last year, it may have been even a little more chaotic than normal. Joey was very loud with his verbal stims (repeated noises, squeaks, squeals, etc.) He was also a little extra bouncy that day. No doubt these behaviors were a result of the extra action at the mall, but he was having a pretty good time.

Anyway, I don't usually notice a lot of strange looks from people, but on this day, they were plentiful. Don't get me wrong, a curious look or a compassionate smile from someone doesn't bother me at all. I understand where the curiosity comes from. But these looks were more looks of irritation and annoyance with my beautiful boy, and this mama bear has absolutely NO patience for that.

So what's a mama bear to do? Of course I was not going to confront these miserable people directly and ruin our day…not my style. Nope. Instead I bought some mistletoe from the dollar store and hung it from my back belt loop, right over my butt.

I don't even know if anyone got my point, but it was enough to make me giggle instead of fume as I felt the eyes following us for the rest of our fun-filled adventure. A mama's gotta do what a mama's gotta do.

59. Honest, Abe. I didn't mean to knock you over!!

Taking Joey to the movie theater is always interesting. Walking in, waiting in line for tickets, smelling the popcorn, watching and listening to all the people...it can be somewhat overwhelming for my boy.

I usually try to take him on less crowded days and times to avoid much of the extra hoopla. On this particular day though, Shayna's second grade teacher was going to meet the kids from her class for a movie on a Saturday afternoon. Such a sweet teacher, meeting her students on her day off. But yep. A crowded day. Hmm. It was also to be the first time that she would meet our Joey.

So there we were, waiting in the fairly long ticket line, when Joey spotted a sign advertising the new "Abraham Lincoln" movie.

It was about 12+ feet tall, a cut out display of good old Honest Abe himself. Joey was fascinated. He touched it. He touched it again. AND THEN...at the exact moment that Shayna's teacher was walking up to us in the line, it happened. He smacked that display just a little too hard, and down, down, down it fell. It was all in slow motion from there.

Thankfully, it was made of cardboard so nobody got hurt,

but the movie theater staff came running over really fast. It was quite an unusual and amusing sight for all that witnessed it. (Well maybe not amusing to the staff, but definitely unusual).

Wow that thing was big! Anyway, my boy sure can make a memorable first impression!! Sheesh.

60. That's not what I meant, you silly boy!!

As I said, trips to the movies with my kiddos are often interesting. On this day, everything had gone just fine. We got our tickets, we had waited for our popcorn, and then we sat down in our seats. No problem.

I was sitting in the middle between my two beautiful babies, as we were getting settled in. Joey was on the aisle, and I asked him to take off his sweatshirt. I then turned my attention to Shayna to help her remove her jacket. When I looked back at my Joey, he was sitting there, innocent as could be, with absolutely NO SHIRT ON!!! Bahahahaha!! I could not believe my eyes!! It was such a surprising sight , that I cannot even fully give it justice here.

Apparently, when I said, "Take off your sweatshirt.", he thought I said to take off his shirt. Too funny!! I will have that image burned into my mind for the rest of my life. In fact, it's one of my go to things when I need a giggle. Man, I love that kid!!

61. I thought this place had a pool!

Being the older brother, Joey has to attend most of his little sister's school shows, dance recitals, etc. Most of the time, he does pretty well, although I always have to have quick exit plan just in case. I am usually well prepared for these events, but there was one particular holiday show at Shayna's school when I was kind of caught off guard.

About 2 weeks prior, I had taken the kids to an indoor pool that was housed inside of a school building. We had a great time, both kids loved it, and I fully intended to make it a regular thing. Flash forward to sitting in the crowded gym at Shayna's school.

Joey started to say, "Swimming please." over and over again. "I want swimming please." My heart was racing, I knew exactly why he thought we were going swimming, but I also knew that not only didn't Shayna's school have a pool, but at that moment, I was fairly certain I was going to miss my daughter's performance. Oy.

I played the distraction game for about a half hour. What is the distraction game, you ask? Well, it involves the use of my bag of tricks that I bring to any activity with Joey. Snacks, toys, water, fidgets, etc. When I know it's going to be a particularly hard thing for him to sit through, I bring the heavy artillery (like chocolate or something), but I didn't anticipate the pool request at this event. Ugh.

As with everything, I was trying to see the positives in the moment. He is so wonderfully verbal when he really wants something, but at the same time, my heart was breaking for him because he didn't understand what was going on. Swimming is his favorite thing in the world, and I never would have put him in that situation on purpose.

He made it through the show just fine, but when it was over and it was time to leave, he was not a happy camper. He just didn't get it, and it made us both really sad. Poor guy. The next day, we went swimming...but never again at the school with a pool.

62. A three ring circus...

I really liked the circus as a kid. The trapeze, the tightrope, the costumes, the music...all of it is very exciting. I love to share my own childhood memories with my kids any chance I get, and what could be better than "The Greatest Show on Earth"?

Again, because Joey is not a big fan of crowds, I decided to get us tickets for a weekday performance, and for the first time ever, I thought of purchasing "disabled seating". This would make it so we could easily access our seats without fighting the crowds. Brilliant!

So I let my babies (I think they were about 8 and 5 at the time) play hooky from school, grabbed my mom, and off we went. I had my bag of tricks, we bought some popcorn, light up toys, and were all set for a great time.

Our seats were awesome. We sat in folding chairs on a cement deck instead of being smushed together in the stadium seating. There was plenty of room to move about, and Joey could even stand up and bounce around a little without bothering anybody. Perfect.

The show was indeed spectacular, and we were all enjoying it very much, UNTIL... I smelled something funny. Not funny ha ha, this was funny yuck yuck. Oh no!! There was no way that I was dragging this somewhat stinky kid through the stadium, down the hall, to who knows where, trying to keep him calm in the crowds, and then attempting to change him on the floor of a public bathroom. Gross.

So what's a mama bear to do? Well, I changed that boy at lightning speed, in the pitch black dark, right there at our seats. I tied that stinky stuff up in a plastic bag, and we continued on with the show!

I was so impressed with myself. We didn't even miss a beat, and nobody around us was even the wiser. A mama's gotta do what a mama's gotta do, right?

We continued with our fun until the very last act...which unfortunately, was the clowns on trampolines. Trampolines are another one of Joey's favorite things in the whole world. So, my sweet boy that is only verbally motivated by highly desirable activities starts to repeat, "I want trampoline please. I want jump please". Over and over again. He wanted to be in the show!! Oy...with some master distractor techniques I dodged that bullet, but it certainly was an interesting day!!

63. Look!! A Polar Bear!!

Watching my kids watch the animals at the zoo warms my heart. I love it. On this particular day, at Shayna's request, we searched for the Polar Bear exhibit for quite a while. We finally found it, and there was a small crowd all watching the polar bears walking around in their habitat.

Every head, little and big, was turned in their direction. Every head that is, but one. My Joey's head was turned the opposite way, looking at the Polar Bear's unoccupied swimming pool. Hahaha!!

64. All terrain mama...

My hubby and I have always loved to walk in the woods. We continued this love as we had our children, and to this day, our favorite path is called "The Snozberry Trail".

From the day we had our kids, we have included them on our walks. When Joey was a baby, I even brought our everyday stroller with us through the muddiest of muddy trails. I would have 2 inches of mud caked up on every tire. That's when Darin started calling me "all terrain mama", because he knew that nothing would stop me from pushing that baby. It was so fun.

When Shayna came along, I would do the same thing with a double stroller! I honestly don't know how I did it!! I sure did earn that nickname!!

It's a lot easier these days, no strollers, just by backpack full of water, bug spray, and food. We still do it whenever we can. It's one of the few family outings that we have that involves very little preparation, and almost no stress. We all love it, and it's FREE!!

65. Recently, on the Snozberry Trail...

Just recently, we went for one of our walks on the good old Snozberry Trail. We have probably done that walk at least a hundred times by now, and each time is quite similar to the time before.

Joey will pick up and carry the biggest stick he can find, Darin and Shayna walk up ahead looking for the next adventure, and Joey and I stay a bit further behind, taking little breaks every so often. The last time though, was bit different for some reason.

Joey was a bundle of energy, running up ahead of all of us for a time. All of these years, I thought I was walking slowly to stay with my boy, but it turns out, maybe I'm just slow! Haha. In any case, what happened next will stay in my heart forever.

Joey ran up ahead again, and when Darin and Shayna caught up to him, they walked down the path a bit.

My sweet and wonderful boy stopped dead in his tracks, turned around to see where I was, and stood there watching...waiting for me to catch up before he would take one more step. Total role reversal...my little protector!!! What a good boy he is...and he sure does love his mama. Sniff sniff.

66. Me, my girl, and a very special night...

I wasn't sure if I was even going to share this story or not, but with all of the stories of bad news, anger, selfishness and greed in this world (that we all hear about daily), I thought it might be nice to help renew a little of everyone's faith in the human race. So here it goes. :-))

We had bought Shayna tickets for a "One Direction" concert as a Christmas/Hanukkah gift way back in November of 2012. The ONLY tickets left for purchase at that time were on the lawn.

Because she is such an awesome kid, the best "big sister" that a little sister ever was, and mostly because she is just an all -around amazing small human being (who has to deal with much more than most kids her age)…I really wanted it to be a special night for us. It would be her very first concert, and she LOVES "One Direction".

I knew she would be SOOO excited, so I snatched up two lawn tickets as fast as I could. She would be looking forward to this concert for the next seven months.

Fast forward to two weeks before the concert. I started feeling kind of sad that our tickets were not so great. With our life being as unpredictable and insane as it is sometimes, she doesn't have many opportunities to have an entire night that is ALL ABOUT HER. I wanted this night to be amazing.

Somehow, this crazy thought came to me, and I decided to send a completely unsolicited email to an extremely influential, quite busy, and apparently very big hearted "high -up" executive in the music industry.

The letter was short and sweet, basically containing the same information that you just read. I asked him if there was any way to "upgrade" our tickets to this long sold out show. I wasn't even sure that I had the right email address, but within an hour or so, he personally wrote me back and said he would see what he could do.

By the next day, his team in Chicago contacted me, and I was told that we would have pavilion tickets waiting for us at "will call" on the day of the show. They said we could exchange our lawn tickets at the box office window, and there would be no extra charge. I was completely blown away.

Fast forward to the night of the concert. Shayna and I arrived at the box office (she still didn't know that we weren't sitting on the lawn…which she thought was called "the yard" SO CUTE!) We picked up our tickets, and they were for the main floor, up close and personal to all the action!! AMAZING!!! We were both squealing with happiness.

At that point, she asked me how we got the tickets… I got totally choked up and told her that some very important people agreed with me that she is a great kid, and that's why they wanted our night to be so special. It was so awesome to tell her that.

Unbelievably awesome seats!! Unbelievably amazing night!! Unbelievably big hearted, wonderful people, making one very special little girl VERY happy. (and her Mama too!!)

So, I hope you smiled reading this, because it's one of those moments that she and I will remember forever. Just wanted to share. Kindness is still alive and well. :-)))

67. Bouncing along in our automobile...

If you are one of those people that assumes a bouncing vehicle can only mean one thing...think again. Our boy is a one man show when we are driving along in my minivan. He LOVES listening to music, and he is quite animated when his favorite songs come on. He bounces along to the beat, shaking the seat, and all of the passengers right along with him.

It doesn't bother me, but since he's gotten bigger, I know that we no longer go unnoticed during stoplights, trains, and the occasional bumper to bumper traffic. But at least my boy knows how to turn a boring old traffic jam into a fun and exciting traffic "JAM". Gotta love it!!

68. The Tire Swing...

I have always tried to make sure that every so often, I get some individual, quality time with each of my kids; Those wonderful moments when they can have one hundred percent of my attention...I love it, and so do they.

One particular day a few years ago, my boy and I headed out for a fun Mama/Joey day. We went out for chicken and french fries (two of his favorite foods), and then headed over to a fort themed playground to enjoy the beautiful afternoon.

We were having a great time, so as I often do, I decided to encourage my Joey to try something new. He loves the swings, so we did that for a bit, but then I wanted him to try the tire swing. Yep...all my brilliant idea.

Anyway, I took his hand, we walked over, and it was too high for him to sit on by himself. It was about waist high on me, pretty high for a tire swing, but I was still able to pick him up at the time, so I helped him climb on in.

He was uncertain at first, and wasn't sure how to sit. After an awkward few seconds of shuffling, he laid down with his butt going through the center, and his arms resting on the sides.

I started to push him, and he was really enjoying it UNTIL...his butt started to sink further and further down into the hole in the center. It all happened so fast, but suddenly, he was TOTALLY stuck!! His chin was touching his chest, his shoulders were bent in, and his butt was sinking way further down. He wouldn't fit all the way through the hole, and he was wedged in there so tight that I couldn't pull him back out the way he got in. I tried to pick up the swing to turn it over and kind of dump him out, but it was too high and awkward for me to get the leverage I needed.

By that point, my poor boy was screaming and crying because it was hurting him, and he was terrified. I was looking around for someone that could possibly help me, but I couldn't see anybody due to the "fort" design of the playground.

I started yelling for help, and was pretty much ready to call 911 when two other moms came running around the corner and helped me get my poor traumatized kid out of that horrible freakin' thing. Oy. What a "special" day that turned out to be!! The poor kid had lines across his back for a few days afterward.

SOOO...let's just say that this mama still harbors a strong dislike for tire swings, and more often than not, now lets her boy take the lead when it comes to choosing playground equipment. Ugh.

69. Haircuts and lollipops...

Up until a year or so ago, the thought of taking Joey to get a professional haircut completely freaked me out. I could not even imagine him sitting in one of those barber chairs, leaving the drape on, or even sitting still for nearly enough time to get the job done. For those reasons, and then some, we would just go ahead and cut it at home. Thankfully, his hair has always been dark, so it was never very obvious when we made it uneven.

One day, as I was cleaning up the HUGE mess of tiny hairs from using the clippers on Joey's thick hair, it dawned on me. I was pretty sure he was ready to take the plunge. Ok...maybe I was the one that was ready, but either way, this kid was going to try the salon next time.

I called ahead, tried my best to explain Joey in a nutshell, and asked if they could please find somebody sweet and patient to help us upon our arrival. They were very accommodating.

So the day came. I had made up several songs about haircuts, with lyrics including the swivel chair, the clippers, the mirrors, etc. I sang to him, and had him fill in the blanks so I knew he would know what to expect.

We walked in, he sat in the chair, and was FANTASTIC!! No problems at all!! That's my boy!! When he was all done, they gave him a lollipop, and I think at that moment, he was hooked.

The only thing is, that now when we go, he wants the lollipop first, and eats it while he's getting the haircut. Kind of a gross sticky mess, but nothing a little wash cloth and baby powder won't fix at the end. Haha.

70. Tall guy in tiny town...

My boy will take a splash in the water any which way he can get it. So when he had a day left of his summer break last year, and Shayna had already gone back to school, I took him to our favorite little sprinkler park.

On previous visits, there were kids of all ages, but on that particular day, apparently all of the big kids had gone back to school. Tiny little toddlers and preschoolers were running about through the park. Well, I should say tiny little toddlers, preschoolers, and one great big gorgeous twelve year old boy!

It was quite a sight to see. He had a great time, and I think the little ones thought he was the coolest kid ever. For those few hours, he was absolutely the titan of tiny town.

***PLEASE NOTE: THE FOLLOWING THREE STORIES ARE IN CHRONOLOGICAL ORDER, AND SHOULD BE READ TOGETHER.

71. Three Little Birds in the ER...(#1 of 3)

Having a child that cannot tell you what is wrong or where they are hurting is absolutely heartbreaking. It's horrible enough that you know they are in pain, but when you don't even know how to make them feel better, the feeling of helplessness is indescribable. Like I said, my guessing abilities are usually pretty good when it comes to my boy, but it's still just a guess.

Joey was about 9 at the time, and was having what I thought were terrible stomach pains. Meltdowns twice an hour or more, all day and night. I was giving him Maalox, Pepto, Gas-X, Rolaids, etc. All would help for a little while, but then he would be in pain again.

I knew I had to have a doctor take a look at him, but I was hardly able to handle him at home in those horrible moments, much less attempting the car or the doctor's office.

So what's a mama bear to do? Well, I called the "drive-thru" doctor to see what she suggested, and she strongly encouraged me to take him to the emergency room. We needed to rule out a couple of things in order to make any progress. Basically, she said we should make sure it wasn't his appendix, and secondly that he didn't ingest something that was causing a blockage of some sort.

Of course, being who I am, both of those things had occurred to me as well, and hearing them from her confirmed that we should indeed go to the ER. But how? OMG. This was a kid that freaked out at the regular doctor's office! How in the world would I get him to cooperate in the emergency room?!?!

The doctor went on to say that she would prescribe a little Xanax for him, and that I should give it to him about 20 minutes before going in. I had never given him anything like that before, but I was scared to death for my sweet boy, and I had to do something. First we would go to Walgreens, and then I would take him to the hospital. Gulp.

When we arrived at the pharmacy drive-thru, my poor kid was just writhing in pain. He was banging on the windows, kicking the seats, screaming, crying, etc. It was so awful. Of course the medicine wasn't ready yet, pffft, so I had to pull around into their parking lot and wait. It seemed like FOREVER, but they finally called and said it was ready. I pulled back into the parking lot, measured out the dose, and gave it to him right there.

He was so miserable, the poor little guy. I drove the ten minutes or so to the hospital parking lot, and waited about another ten minutes. He calmed down some, and we walked inside. I told them a little bit about Joey, and that we would need to take things kind of slowly and quietly with him. They were very nice.

One of my own favorite calming songs has always been "Three Little Birds" by Bob Marley. It works for me, and I figured it might work for my boy as well. So I started singing.

He loved it, and kept asking for it again and again, and again.

SOOOO…about six hours later, after about 10,000 renditions of "Three Little Birds", an x-ray, a blood test, and assorted pokes and prods, they still weren't sure what was wrong with my boy, but they did know it was not an infection of any kind, not his appendix, and not a blockage. Phew.

He was AMAZING through the whole ordeal. They sent us home with some kind of prescription tummy medicine, and told us to follow up with a GI doctor. At least he seemed to be feeling better. The painful "episodes" came and went for the next few weeks while we waited for our appointment…Of course our trips to the GI doctor would prove to be interesting as well. TO BE CONTINUED...

72. Seriously?? A "consultation"??? Did you hear me at all??? (#2 of 3)

Finding a GI doctor that also had some knowledge on autism proved to be next to impossible. Why? I don't know! Kids with autism often have gut issues, yet nobody could help us? So frustrating. Anyway, I finally got an appointment for a "consultation" at Children's Memorial. I knew that a "consultation" was beyond a stupid waste of time, but apparently I had no choice but to jump through their hoops and hurdles if I ever wanted to figure out what was wrong with my son... SOOOO off we went to our "consultation" downtown.

In the office, the doctor asked me all kinds of questions, and of course, as I had very clearly explained to them on the phone, I was not able to completely focus on talking to them because Joey was into everything in the room.

They seemed to know nothing about autism, and were not the able to grasp the fact that Joey could not tell me what was bothering him. UGH.

Finally, after a bunch of gobbly gook, they agreed that he needed to have a scope performed. Hallelujah! Finally we would actually be able to SEE what was going on in there.

We made our next appointment to meet them at the

hospital on a future date. Joey would need to be there very early in the morning, without eating, and they were going to have to knock him out. It all scared the crap out of me, but I knew it had to be done. We would have the procedure in about three weeks...

73. Can you please just knock me out too? Pretty please?? (#3 of 3)

We decided that it would be better to stay downtown the night before the procedure to avoid any potential problems that could arise early in the morning. We live about an hour and a half away from that hospital, and Joey was not allowed to eat or drink anything until we were all done. So I thought it would be best to stay nearby, wake him up a little later, and go straight over.

My stress level was already so high, that I asked my mom to come with Joey and I instead of Darin. I love my husband dearly, but sometimes he can add extra stress, and between Joey's stress level and mine, I just couldn't risk it. So that was the plan. A nice relaxing evening at the hotel, watching TV in bed, and up early for an easy trip to the hospital.

Well, we got to the hotel just fine, but apparently it was built a VERY long time ago. The room was a crazy odd shape. Such an odd shape that you couldn't even see the TV from either bed.

I finally moved the bed over a bit so we could see part of it, but turned on the TV to find that the only channel that came in was airing some infomercial with girls in bikinis selling some sort of stupid product. Seriously??

I called downstairs to complain, but when they knocked on the door to come fix it, Joey got upset and I had to ask them to leave. Oh the joy!

At least my boy seemed to enjoy the girls on the TV, but me?? Not so much.

Morning came eventually, and we headed off to the hospital. We had to sit and wait for a while when they were checking us in. Everything seemed to be going fine UNTIL...my boy, that was not allowed to eat or drink anything that morning, found an old, chewed up piece of gum stuck to the bottom of his chair, and yes...popped it into his mouth!!!! OMG!!!! Not just old dirty gum from some stranger, old dirty gum from some stranger that was stuck to the bottom of a chair in a hospital for who knows how many germ collecting years!!!! YUCK!!! UGH!!!!!

Finally, they called us up, they got him ready, and I went back to the operating room with him until they knocked him out. I was such a nervous wreck that I couldn't even speak. I couldn't drink the coffee my mom handed me. I couldn't sit down, but I wasn't comfortable standing either. It was excruciatingly awful. But...according to the clock, it was only about a half hour later when the doctor came out to talk to me. (It felt like hours to me!)

Joey had an ulcer. An ULCER!! Poor baby!! No wonder he was so miserable!!! On the one hand, I was mortified that he had this problem, but on the other hand, I was so relieved that I hadn't been WAY off in left field about what had been bothering him. It was his tummy, and somehow I knew!! Thank goodness.

Prescriptions in hand, we left the hospital, the ulcer healed up nicely, and I earned a couple more of those mama stripes. Always an adventure.

74. Lighting it up blue...

April is autism awareness month. Several years ago, Autism Speaks created the "Light it up Blue" campaign, bringing some much needed attention to all of us that live this life daily.

International landmarks around the world join in and show their support on the second day of April every year. We change our outdoor light bulbs from clear to blue, and ask family members, friends, neighbors, local schools, community buildings, etc. to do the same.

At our house, we leave it up for the entire month. Now I am asking you. Do you light it up blue? I hope so...it's a little something that you can do to warm somebody's heart. Autism can seem like a lonely world sometimes, and it's always nice to see that people are willing to make a little effort to show their support.

75. Shoes, boots, hats, and gloves...

Thirteen years into this, and I still have no answers to these problems. I'm always trying something new. Maybe someday I'll become an autism fashion designer? Probably not.

76. These boots aren't made for walkin'...

Where do I begin...hmm. Ok, well, Joey loves to touch the snow, he loves to play with it, taste it, roll around in it, and even put his face right in it! Sounds like he loves it, right? Yes, he does, but there's a problem.

You see, my son will NOT leave his hat on his head, his boots on his feet, or his mittens on his hands. He ends up completed unprotected form the cold. SOO...like clockwork, I spend a half hour getting the poor kid all bundled up, he steps outside, starts to play, takes everything off within five minutes, and then gets really mad because he is so uncomfortable.

This has happened year after year after year since he was about two. Ugh. I have attempted so many different creative techniques to get him to keep that stuff on.

A few examples include: knee socks stretched over his hands and all the way up his arms, all placed under his jacket to be used as mittens. Boots that lace up high under his snow pants so in theory, he can't get them off. Hats that fit comfortably over or even around his headphones, with ties tied tightly under his chin, scarves tied around his neck and mouth in an attempt to at least keep his face warm...and countless other little tricks over the years, all to no avail.

Last year, he finally decided he wasn't going to play in the snow anymore. I couldn't even get him to come outside after I got him all bundled up. Poor guy. :-(I'm not giving up though, we'll be trying again soon.

77. No, Mama. I like my shoes like this...

How does my boy like his shoes, you ask? He likes to step on the backs until they are completely smushed down, making it impossible to securely place the shoe on his foot.

Sometimes high tops work for a little while, but this mama has found that backless, slip on shoes usually make more sense for Joey. They aren't as sturdy or warm as I would like, but at least they are designed to stay on his feet. I'll take what I can get.

78. I want French fries please...

My kid has always loved his French fries, and because of this, I have used them as a reward on more than one occasion.

For example, I might tell him, "FIRST shopping. THEN French fries". This usually works out well, but there is one time that comes to mind, where it did not.

We had gone out to run a bunch of errands, and Joey asked me for his beloved treat. I told him that we would get them, but only when errands were "all done". I had to remind him many times ..."FIRST we finish errands. THEN we get French fries."

Somehow, he kept it together during our longer that normal run, and eventually ,we made it to the drive-thru at the golden arches.

We pulled up, ordered, went to the first window, paid, and THEN IT HAPPENED. The dreaded words that the person at the window spoke to me sent shivers of terror up and down my spine. "The fries are not ready yet, please pull up into the space ahead and wait".

OMG!!! ARE YOU FREAKIN' KIDDING ME??? This had never happened to me with Joey in the car. I knew there was going to be trouble. We pulled up to the spot, and my sweet and confused boy started repeating, "French fries please. French fries please. FRENCH FRIES PLEASE!!" and off the handle he flew.

Huge meltdown in the car, not understanding why we had gone through the whole process of the drive-thru, and still did not have any food. Poor baby.

By the time she brought our food out to us, he was way beyond the point of no return. It took him about 20 minutes to calm down, but eventually, he did eat his French fries, even though they were cold.

That was such a bum deal. There was no way to see that one coming. Never a dull moment I guess.

79. A random act of kindness...

Over the Summer, we took the kids to a county fair. It's always a risk at these types of things, but I don't want to deprive any of us of some good old fashioned family fun, so sometimes, I just have to go for it and hope for the best. Yes, a fair and carnival does have a lot of crowds and noise, but there's also a lot of food, and this works out well for my Joey.

I don't put him on many rides because he can be quite unpredictable. If he were to have a meltdown, touch , eat or chew something he shouldn't, or try to get up, etc. etc. etc...it's just not worth the risk. If there's something that one of us can go on with him, we're willing, but Joey doesn't usually want to go anyway.

UNTIL... we walked by this amazingly awesome looking bouncy, bungee, flying thing at that county fair. It DEFINITELY caught his eye, and mine too for that matter. I had to investigate a little further.

I had Darin and the kids go sit down with a nice little distracting snack, and I walked over to the tattooed, biker looking carnival guy to ask him some questions. I had to figure out if I thought Joey could do the "X-treme Jump" thing safely, before we invested the time and money into starting the whole process.

Turned out that the carnival guy had a nephew with autism, and he wanted to let both of my kids jump for free!! This big guy was so sweet and patient with Joey too. What a doll, and of course both kids LOVED it!!

That sweet man wouldn't even let me tip him, or buy him food, or anything. He said it was his good deed for the day. What a great experience. I so love and appreciate those rare moments when everything works out!! So fun!!!

80. Disabled? Hmmm...

Whenever we go anywhere, I always do my best to transition us in and out without any huge hurdles. I must also develop a quick getaway plan in case such a plan becomes necessary. Most of the time, these plans end with a trip back to our car.

Anyway, in the past, sometimes the car was REALLY far away, making for a challenging walk to and from the parking lot. Particularly challenging when weather was bad, or when handling a large child in the middle of a meltdown.

So what's a mama bear to do? Well, let me tell you, one day I had a revelation. My son has a disability. Of course I already knew that, but I never actually HEARD myself say it. My son has a DISABILITY. Isn't there special parking for disabled people?? Yes, there is!!! Haha.

What a game-changer for us. SO many things have become at least a little bit easier because we can now utilize those closer spaces. I cannot even tell you how helpful that has been. Yay!

81. Joey and the chocolate factory...

Two years ago, near the end of summer break, my mom & I took the kids on a tour of a local chocolate factory. It smelled so yummy in there and it was a lot of fun. Anyway, part of the tour included this little "chocolate museum" of sorts. Inside of tall, clear case (hopefully sturdy) there was a 1000 pound chocolate statue. Joey was literally hugging the outside of this case, with his tongue pressed against the glass. Pretty funny. We all wanted to do the same thing, but Joey was the brave one. Haha. Chocolate love is hereditary I guess.

82. The fireworks and the funeral home...

We live in a boating town, but for seemingly obvious reasons, we do not own a boat. This does not usually present a problem for us, but for a few times in the summer.

Our town has a few fireworks displays every year, and there's only a handful of places to watch them if you don't have a boat. That being the case, the few restaurants/bars on the water get VERY crowded and loud, and there is no way I would even try to bring Joey inside.

So what's a mama bear to do? Well, a couple times, we tried to find a neighborhood that we could see from, but that didn't work out so well. Too many trees. The next year, I decided to drive near the restaurant that they were shooting them off from, to see if we could park nearby.

Everything was packed and overflowing, UNTIL...I saw the roped off parking lot behind the funeral home. It looked like there was a family down by the water, getting ready to watch the show. I pulled up to a lady that was kind of guarding the rope, and I asked her if we could please pull into their lot. I told her about Joey, and his dislike of crowds, and she let us right in.

It turned out that the family that was sitting back there owns the funeral home. They were very nice to us and let us watch the show with them.

It's so hard to explain, but sometimes the smallest act of kindness from a stranger is enough to ease the pain caused by some of the ding dongs that we all have to deal with. There are sweet people out there, sometimes you just have to look a little harder to find them.

83. Joey and Mama are lost in the woods. Uh oh...

I love walking in the woods, but I never do it by myself, and until this particular day, I had never gone alone with either of my kids. In fact, you know this will be an interesting story, because I haven't done it since either. Hmm.

Anyway, one crisp spring day, my brain was just feeling too overloaded with life. I needed to get to some nature and decompress. So I grabbed my boy, and off to the woods we went.

Now Darin doesn't ever want me to go to the woods alone, but we had been to this particular park many times, and had even had one of Shayna's birthday parties there. There is a nature center, and even some staff around. So we were both ok with it.

When we had gone before, we always chose the path around the bog. It is a boardwalk type walk, and it's only about a mile. On this day though, I was in the mood to try something new. I knew there was a walking trail through the woods if we walked the other way, so that's what I decided to do.

It was great for a while. We walked through big muddy puddles with our boots, we found cool sticks, listened to the birds, etc. It was just what I needed. We were both enjoying our time together very much UNTIL...I suddenly realized that we had been walking for quite a long time, and there seemed to be no end in sight. Hmm.

Walking, walking, walking. No sign of where we had come in... Uh oh. Where the heck were we? I could see a familiar water tower in the very far distance, but that didn't help me to get my bearings. My feet were starting to hurt, and we had already finished our one bottle of water.

I kept thinking that we would come to an exit at any moment, but we didn't. On the plus side, I definitely stopped thinking about the other problems that had been on my mind. Ugh.

On and on and on we walked. It became a bit scary at that point, because I knew that Joey didn't have much more in him, and handling a meltdown in the middle of the woods, by myself, would not be pretty. Gulp. Great job, Mama. Oops.

Eventually, we found our way back to the car without any huge issues. We have gone for many walks, but before that particular day, I don't think we had ever gone more than a mile or two. Apparently, in my excitement to try something new, I missed the fairly large sign that said that the path we were about to take was almost 4 miles long!!! Oy!! Duh.

It's a funny memory now, but it was pretty darn scary while it was happening. That is why these days, we stick to family walks in the woods. Tee hee.

84. What do you mean there are no apples at "The Apple Store"??

I take a ton of pictures with my iPhone. My cloud is always full, I have thousands of pictures on there, and I often run out of memory. So the first time this happened, I freaked because I thought I was going to lose all of my pictures.

I had to go to The Apple Store to see what needed to be done. It happened to be a day that Joey was off school, so he and I had been out having some fun. He was ready to have lunch, but I told him, FIRST we have to go to The Apple Store, and THEN lunch. He was cooperative, so in we went.

It's kind of busy in those stores, and there are a lot of wires and things that caught Joey's attention for a few minutes. The guy came over to help us, and it took a little time for him to explain what I needed to do.

Joey was standing near me of course, and then started to say "Apple please. I want apple please." OMG!! I didn't even think about how ridiculous this entire scenario must have seemed to him. He absolutely LOVES apples, and I hadn't even put two and two together that he might think we were going to a real apple store!! How cute is he??

I was trying so hard not to laugh, Of course they should have apples at The Apple Store! Duh!! When we were finished, we went to the grocery store to get our lunch (Including apples of course).

85. Was it Zorro or Joey?...

My family and extended family love cake. We have it for every holiday, special occasion, get together, etc. If nobody specifies what to bring, we will end up with 5 of them.

Well, for about 8 years, from around age 2 until about age 10, every time we had a cake around for a family party, Joey would make a mad dash for it, swiping his hand over the top, getting a premature taste of frosting.

It would leave this funny imprint that only my Joey could have made. It always reminded me of the "Z" that Zorro would make with his sword. Oy. That's my boy...Mama likes cake too.

86. Another nice guy...

I took my boy to one of those crazy sports trampoline places to have a little fun on a day off from school. It was our first time, so I really didn't know what to expect. When we walked in, I quickly realized that this was not a place that Joey was going to be comfortable.

I didn't realize that all of the kids go on all of the trampolines. I kind of thought that each child would be assigned their own, but apparently that's not how it works. Everyone goes everywhere and it is crazy, loud, and chaotic. He LOVES to jump, but I could see that this scenario was setting him up for disaster.

Walking a little further inside, I noticed that there was one section that was completely blocked off for the day. It had about ten empty trampolines, and nobody was allowed to use them. I took my boy up to the front desk, explained my concerns, and asked if we could please use the roped off area. HE SAID YES!!! YAY!!!

Joey had ten trampolines all to himself, and he had an absolutely fabulous time. What a lucky boy!! Love those random acts of kindness!!

87. The ring bearer and the flower girl...oy!

Years ago, when Joey was seven and Shayna was four, my baby cousin was getting married. She was sweet and asked all four of us to be a part of her special day. Darin and I were to be in the bridal party, and Joey and Shayna were to be the ring bearer and flower girl.

Sounds lovely doesn't it? Yes, of course, but my crazy life tends to be a bit more complicated than that of your average bear (or "bearer" as it were).

Of course shopping for the beautiful dress for Shayna was a lot of fun, but choosing the right outfit for Joey was another story. All of the groomsmen were renting their tuxedos from a formal wear shop. They had Joey's size, but I knew that if I rented him a tuxedo, he would likely destroy it, and we would be stuck paying them a lot of money that we didn't have. So I decided to cut out the middle man and just buy him one. At least that way, I could hunt for a bargain.

So, we found him the tux, the tie, and the shoes, and I crossed my fingers that he would keep them in decent condition until after he walked down the aisle. (Well, at least until after he was "supposed to" walk down the aisle...I had my doubts about how well that was going to go).

Ok...we were ready. Time went by, and it was the day of the rehearsal dinner. As always, I was nervous about how Joey would behave, but I had my bag of tricks, and hoped for the best.

He was pretty good at the rehearsal...my little four year old Shayna took her brother's hand and they walked down the aisle together. I was to walk right after them just in case there were any mishaps. It went pretty well. I was so nervous that he might have an aggressive meltdown in the middle of everything, but so far, so good.

My stress level was really high the next day. Darin and I were arguing, I had to pack overnight bags and include everything we would need to get ready for the wedding at the hotel, and apparently our gas had been shut off due to a late payment, and therefore none of the laundry had dried in the dryer overnight.

I would have to keep Joey away from the bride just in case

he should decide to scratch her, leaving a big puffy pink line down her chest, or play with something on her dress or veil, causing something to break. Yikes. What the hell was I thinking??? I was SOOOOO stressed.

Darin and I were arguing so much that I decided to take the kids in my car and have him meet us down at the hotel a little later. I needed to breathe for a minute. So, the kids and I met my sister down at the hotel, and she even had a beer waiting for me. Love her.

We sat in our room for what seemed like only a few minutes, when my phone rang. It was my loving husband (lol) who had just completely lost the brakes in his car on the way down to the hotel. WHAT??? Are you kidding me???? Ugh.

My sister was nice enough to go pick him up while I stayed at the hotel with the kids. Thank GOD the kids and I were not in that car with him!!! Sheesh. They made it back safely, Darin got dressed and joined the boys, my sister, Shayna and I went to get ready with the girls, and my mom was sweet enough to stay in the room with Joey until it was time for the wedding.

Ten minutes or so before "go time", I came back to the room to get my boy all dressed up in his tuxedo. So handsome!!

The next twenty minutes or so were very chaotic and stressful. We had to take the elevator to the floor where the wedding would take place, walk through the crowded hallways, and eventually wait for everything to begin.

My boy was feeling the stress in the air. He was fine for a little while UNTIL…one too many things going on and he started to chew on his shirt, and prepare for battle. OH NO!!! We were supposed to be walking toward the aisle right at that moment!!

We weren't quite passed the point of no return yet…so I handed him a sucker, he started to eat it, and calmed down. I took both of my babies by the hand and walked them down that aisle with me. Smiling pretty the whole way. Phew!!! That was crazy!!!!!!!!

We all had a good time the rest of the night. A million other little arrangements had been made to keep my boy happy throughout dinner etc., and they all worked out pretty well. That was one crazy weekend, I tell ya!! Many more mama stripes earned.

88. Lessons learned...

A couple years later, my sister was getting married. This was to be a much simpler affair, but my stress level was high nonetheless. This time, I decided to have one of Joey's former assistants from school (and one of our favorite people) come with us to the wedding.

She was there to keep an eye on him while the rest of us were busy with wedding stuff. He was happy, I was happy, and I didn't have to have anyone in my family miss anything. Much better.

89. Ghosts of Hanukkah/ Christmas past...

I have always loved the holiday season. Growing up Jewish, we celebrated Hanukkah, but we were never allowed to have a Christmas tree. We weren't hugely religious or anything, and Santa always came to our house on Christmas morning, but no tree. Hmmm. I don't know either.

But anyway, as a teenager, I started decking out my room for Christmas. I bought a little tree, hung stockings, tinsel, lights and pretty much anything I could get my hands on. My friends and family (including Darin when he entered the picture) started calling me "Suzanne-A-Claus", and the rest is history.

So now, fast forward to having our own kids. We still celebrate Hanukkah, Joey's birthday is December 22, and Darin isn't Jewish, so I have the best excuse to go ahead and have a huge and awesome Christmas tree too (aka Joey's birthday tree).

In our house, I refer to the season as "Birth-Hanu-Mas". I love that time of year!!

90. Merry Christmas to all, and to all a...GOODBYE!!

Holidays are easier for me if I just do them at our house. It's a lot of work, but at least we are home, and I don't have to hover over Joey every second. He can go up to his room if he needs a break, and I can actually socialize instead of sitting off in a quiet room somewhere with my boy.

The year he had the ulcer (but we didn't know yet) was the most challenging to date. I tried to plan things a little differently, keeping the family on one side of the house so my boy could have more space to chill. He had been such a wreck, that I wasn't at all sure how he was going to be with all of the extra people and noise in the house.

His birthday had even been awful, and that was just the four of us at his favorite indoor pool. Obviously, the poor guy was not feeling very well.

He was great for a couple hours. UNTIL...He must have

had a sudden burst of pain because my poor boy just suddenly lost it. I had to take him upstairs, and soon Thereafter, had to ask my family to leave. They all knew that this was a possibility before they came over, but it was still a pretty big bummer. Poor guy.

91. Another random funny...

One afternoon, fairly recently, Shayna asked me for a cookie. I said sure, and asked her to bring one up to Joey.

She came back laughing, and said that when she handed him the cookie, she had asked him, "What do you say?" and he answered, "Bye". Hahaha!! Perfect!! Love my babies!!

92. Happy birthday dear, Joey...

Our boy does NOT like to be the center of attention, he doesn't like noisy crowded places, and he's not much for organized games and/or activities. For these reasons, and many more, we always celebrate his birthdays in "Joey style".

For as long as I can remember, we have taken the kids to some sort of swimming activity during the day, and then come home for pizza and cake at our house (usually with a few extra family members). It's perfect.

Well, last year, I had what I thought was a BRILLIANT idea!! I booked the four of us a room at one of those indoor waterpark resorts, and it was only 30 minutes away from our house. I called ahead to speak to the manager, as I often do, to request some specific accommodations to meet our special needs. I asked for early check-in, a room on the first floor so we wouldn't bother anybody in the room under ours (boing boing boing), and a room closer to the pool so we wouldn't have to go far to give Joey a break.

It was not an inexpensive undertaking, and I wanted everything to go smoothly. The day was fabulous. We swam, ate, played, and had all kinds of fun. By nine o'clock or so, we were all completely exhausted. In fact, Darin and I joked that we should just go home and let someone else have the room for the night, but we were just kidding. Turns out, that would have been a great idea.

I learned a lot of lessons that night: 1) It had been a long time since the four of us had slept in the same room. 2) I may be used to my husband's chainsaw snore, but Joey will NEVER be. 3) A pull out couch for my son sounds like a better idea than it is. 4) An uncomfortable pull out couch, next to the loud hotel room heater, sharing a room with me, my snoring husband and my sweet but overtired and chit chatty daughter, does not make for a happy Joey. 5) If we were ever to "travel" together again, we MUST have a suite with a separate bedroom for my boy. Ugh.

That night was just awful. Meltdown after meltdown. Darin wanted to leave, but there was no way I could safely bring my beautiful but completely overtired and out of control kid down a long hotel hallway at two o'clock in the morning. Finally, he fell asleep at about 3:00am. I stayed up until we finally left at about 6:00. No lovely breakfast. No more swimming. We were done.

This year, my plan is to take him to a hotel with a nice quiet pool, (10 minutes from our house), have fun for the day, use our room for breaks, snacks, and changing... and then go home. We may not be "normal" but we sure are interesting!!

93. 'Cause you're both mine, I walk the line...

Shayna's birthday parties create a completely different set of issues. She LOVES to have a big party with a lot of friends, activities, and fun. She also loves her brother very much, and wants him to be there to celebrate with her.

So what's a mama bear to do? Hmm. Well, it takes a lot of thought, creativity and strategic planning, but I have to say, for the most part, I have been able to pull it off. (at least until her ninth, but I'll get into that a little later).

When Shayna turned four, we had her party in a familiar fast food play area, with a gluten free birthday cake that my boy marked as Zorro. When she turned five, we had her party in our backyard, and the April rain showers actually held off until THE moment the party was over.(There was no way it would have gone well with all of those screaming kids INSIDE...phew) When she turned six, we rented a shelter at the woods and took all of her friends on a nature walk. When she turned seven, we had a pizza party at a local restaurant, 5 minutes from our house, but Joey and Daddy had to miss that one at the last minute because of that poor kid's tummy. When she turned eight, we had a gymnastics party...that was the best. We all had a great time, and Joey was able to jump happily on the trampolines while all the other little people ran around.

THEN...There was the ninth birthday party. She wanted a bowling party. Hmm. Crowded on the weekends, noisy to say the least, and not really in Joey's comfort zone at all. But, we could do this, it would just take some thought.

The bowling alley that Shayna and I like has a "cosmic bowling" side where there are couches instead of chairs, the lights are dim, and they play music videos on huge television screens. Joey had been there before, but only on a weekday afternoon, never on a crowded weekend.

We would be given one hour of bowling, and then one hour in the "party room" for pizza, cake, and presents. They also have a game room.

I actually convinced the manager to let us have the party at 10:30 on a Sunday morning, in hopes of avoiding much of the noise and crowds to keep Joey a little more comfortable. (They usually don't book their first party of the day until noon).

The day came and we set off for the party. This was the first time that it was "girls only" (except for Joey) and Shayna and her friends were having a great time. Joey had found a comfy spot on one of the couches and was playing with some balloons. (He doesn't like to bowl... he'll use the little "ramp" if I help him, but he doesn't enjoy it, so I was just letting him do his thing). He appeared to be relaxed, and it was just about time to move in to the party room.

Everything was going just fine UNTIL... I asked all of the girls to come over and take a picture with Joey. WHAT WAS I THINKING????? I would have gotten so mad at anybody else that would have done that to my poor kid. He was NOT happy. He started chewing on his shirt and hitting and scratching the heck out of me. He actually bit me on my arm, and he never does that!!

I yelled for Darin and we ran with him to the public restroom, hoping he could calm himself down. If nothing else, at least I am pretty quick at implementing our escape plan. At least most of Joey's issues were not on public display.

Ugh. ME??? ME!!???? With all of the thinking and planning that I did for this party, I was the one that did something stupid!! Ugh. I felt so bad, and I still do.

He probably would have calmed down, but Darin decided to take him home. I went back to join the party feeling quite mentally and physically exhausted. Thankfully though, Shayna didn't skip a beat, and continued to have a great time with her friends.

She was glad that Joey and Daddy didn't miss the whole party, and she still wants him there again next time. Perhaps this mama will be having a nice glass of wine before the next party? Perhaps. Hmmm.

94. The Joey, the jousting, and the red knight...

Before having our kids, Darin and I had been to Medieval Times on more than one occasion. I had gone with some friends in high school as well, and it was always a great time. It's a very cool place. Expensive...but cool.

I was forever trying to figure out a way to take our kids there. Every mother's day I would think about it, and every time I would chicken out because it was too expensive, (especially considering the fact that some or all of us might have to wait out in the car for a significant portion of the dinner and show).

Anyway, I was turning 40 last year, and I had the idea again. I realized at that point that if I wasn't going to bite the bullet for my fortieth birthday, I was never going to do it. So...I had to think. Hmmm. Ok...bribery!!

We ended up bringing one of Joey's FAVORITE people in the whole wide world with us, just in case. I bribed him by paying for half of his ticket. He's one of his former assistants from school, and they truly love each other.

We ended up with great seats, great food, and a great time. Sometimes just having a safety net is enough to ensure that you won't need it.

95. Trick or Treat...

I am always walking that line between depriving Joey of something that he may enjoy, and pushing him into doing something that I know he will likely have a hard time with. Halloween is one of those things.

He doesn't seem to care much about dressing up, or trick or treating, but my boy sure does LOVE his candy. So finally, maybe two years ago, I realized that if I just let him eat the candy while we're trick or treating, he'll enjoy himself a whole lot more!! Sometimes it's the simple things I guess.

96. The family camping "retreat" with Joey's school...

When Joey was a baby, we would take him camping and it was a lot of fun. He was only about six months old the first time, and of course it was freezing and raining all night long, but we were all snuggled up in our little tent...and I loved it. We took him a few more times in those early years, and it was always fun.

When Shayna came along, things had gotten a little more complicated, and we couldn't safely tent camp anymore. We did the cabin thing once or twice, but the whole production just got to be too hard for me.

Fast forward to last spring. Joey brought home a flyer from school, telling us that there was going to be a "Family Retreat" camping weekend. I was SOOOO excited!! We would have support from his school staff, and it would be a chance to really bond with some other families. I signed us up right away.

As the date grew closer, I started to panic a little. Hadn't I already decided that the four of us would NEVER try to sleep in the same room again?? Didn't I already know that we needed some sort of "suite" next time?? Well, I had just booked us a room in a cabin to be shared with other families...and not only were all four of us going to be in the same room, but we were going to be sleeping on bunk beds!?!?!? WHAT WAS I THINKING???

I called Joey's favorite former assistant from his school (the same one that came to Medieval Times with us and babysits once in a while) and asked him if he would be going. He is so awesome and said that if we were going, he was going. LOVE HIM!!

So off we went. It was about a two hour ride, and the place was beautiful. We found our room, brought our stuff inside, and started to enjoy ourselves. UNTIL...my poor boy's eyes started watering, he started sneezing, and his face got all puffy. Oh no!!

He had never had seasonal allergies before, but I guess there was something in those woods that my poor kid was terribly allergic to. Oy. Really? What a bum deal.

Well anyway, being a relatively seasoned camper, I had Benadryl in my bag of tricks just in case anybody got stung or something. It helped a little. We muddled through the day with no big issues, and I was trying to relax and think positively about the sleeping arrangements for the evening.

It turned out that the family that was supposed to have the room right next to ours, didn't show up. Hmm. I went to the school staff and asked if we could use that room, and they said YES!! Woo Hoo!! That was a bit of a relief.

As bed time grew closer though, I realized that I had forgotten Joey's melatonin. He takes melatonin just about every day to help regulate his sleep cycle. I FORGOT IT??? ARE YOU KIDDING?? We were in the middle of nowhere, and there was no way that I could run out and buy some. CRAP!!! You would not believe the stuff that I brought on this trip. I had EVERYTHING for EVERY scenario....except for the most important one!!!!! SLEEP!!! Duh, Suz!!!!! Ugh.

So what's a mama bear to do? This kid was probably not going to fall asleep very easily. Oh and a side note, apparently the Benadryl had an energizing effect on my boy, because he was acting all kinds of nuts.

I put Joey to "bed" in one of the rooms, Darin fell asleep in the other, and Shayna and I laid on a couch right outside the door, listening to Joey NOT sleep for several hours. Darin was snoring so loudly in the extra room next door, that I was sure he was going to keep everyone in the entire cabin awake.

Eventually, Joey was quiet, but Shayna and I stayed up giggling, and we definitely didn't want to wake our sleeping boy.

We stayed on that couch all night, while one of our boys had a quiet room, and the other boy sounded like he had a chainsaw running in his. Yes...I now think that our little family of four may need to rent an entire house when we "travel". Sheesh....

97. That wasn't an apple!!!

Why do we only have plastic Christmas tree ornaments? Well, that would be because one time, my sweet boy apparently took big bite out of a shiny red glass ornament, thinking it was an apple. Good times. Ugh.

98. The trampoline and the Tootsie Roll bank...

Just a helpful note to parents out there. If you ever buy your kid an exercise trampoline to open on Christmas morning, you might not want to give them a Tootsie Roll bank that year.

My boy jumped happily on his new trampoline for a few minutes, stepped off right onto the Tootsie Roll bank, and twisted his ankle terribly. I had to run him to the ER before company came for Christmas.

We made it back with time to spare. Thank goodness it wasn't broken, but it was still a little too exciting for me!

99. I will make you love opening presents, young man!!

Joey never really cared about opening presents. He always acted as if I was making him do something that he didn't want to do, as if it was "work". Hmmm.

Well, my boy LOVES yummy snacks, so over the years, I have learned that if I wrap up a few strong smelling, yummy snacks and sneak them into his pile of presents, he is much more motivated to open them. I am one sneaky mama. Tee hee.

100. Hula Hula...

As with most special occasions, I have to plan things wisely in order to have any chance of Joey being successful. My parents' fiftieth wedding anniversary was no exception.

We had to have some sort of party, but as usual money was tight, and Joey was Joey, so what's a mama bear to do? I wanted it to be extra special, not just our usual family get together.

My parents have always loved Hawaii. They have been there a few times, and I think it will always hold a special place in their hearts.

We lived in Florida on their twenty-fifth anniversary, and my brother, sister, and I rented a limo and took them to a fancy Hawaiian dinner and show. It was a lot of fun. But now, for their fiftieth, we live in the mid-west, and I wasn't at all sure something like that even existed around here.

Hmm. Ok, maybe I could do a Luau in my yard. That would be good. Nope...WAYYY too expensive. I actually found a restaurant!! They even had a 5:00 dinner and show, which meant that we actually had a decent chance of Joey being up to the challenge.

The day came, and he was FANTASTIC. He loved the dancers and the food, was there for everything, and had a great time with all of us. It was just another example to prove to myself that where there's a will, there's a way. I will never give up on my sweet boy. It's not always easy, and things don't always work out the way I want them to, but when they do...there's nothing better in the whole world!!!

101. "Autism makes our family special because...." By: Shayna Mitchell (age 10)

Autism makes me special because...I get to do things no one else gets to do.

Autism makes my Daddy special because...it makes him work harder.

Autism makes my Mama special because...it made her write this book.

Autism makes my brother special because...he makes people think about things differently.

Autism makes my family special because...we're different and that's ok.

This page will self-destruct in 5, 4, 3, 2, 1....KABOOM!!

The End. ☺

Made in the USA
Lexington, KY
05 March 2018